YALE JUDAICA SERIES

VOLUME XXVII

THE MIDRASH ON PROVERBS

The Midrash on

Proverbs

. . .

Translated from the Hebrew

with an introduction and annotations by

Burton L. Visotzky

YALE UNIVERSITY PRESS
NEW HAVEN AND LONDON

Designed by James J. Johnson. Set in Sabon
Roman types by Brevis Press, Bethany, Con-
necticut. Printed in the United States by
BookCrafters, Inc., Chelsea, Michigan.

The paper in this book meets the guidelines
for permanence and durability of the Com-
mittee on Production Guidelines for Book
Longevity of the Council on Library
Resources.

10   9   8   7   6   5   4   3   2   1

*Library of Congress
Cataloging-in-Publication Data*

Midrash Proverbs. English.
  The Midrash on Proverbs / translated
from the Hebrew with an introduction
and annotations by Burton L. Visotzky.
  p.   cm. — (Yale Judaica series ; v. 27)
  Translation of: Midrash Proverbs.
  Includes bibliographical references and
index.
  ISBN 0-300-05107-7
  1. Bible. O.T. Proverbs—Commentaries. I. Visotzky, Burton L. II. Title.
III. Series: Yale Judaica series ; 27.
BM517.M77E5   1992
296.1′4—dc20   91-22071

CONTENTS

. . .

INTRODUCTION

· · ·

The term Midrash designates a vast body of literature as well as a process of textual exegesis. Textual exegesis employs a series of hermeneutic norms that have, at various times and places, been applied to biblical texts to search for their contemporary meanings. The compilations of such comments, combined with moral homilies, legends of the sages and saints, and general notices of the effect of global events upon the fortunes of the Jewish people—all these make up the literature called Midrash. This literature constantly meditates on the Bible and on the workings of God in the world. And because God, according to the sages of the Midrash, continually has been involved in the lives of the people Israel, this literature spans millennia of Jewish history and traverses the globe.[1]

Rather than survey a literature that properly begins with the Bible's textual explications (for example, the etymologies of proper names in the book of Genesis) and is carried onward to this day (as in Thomas Mann's *Joseph and His Brothers* or in Margaret Atwood's *Handmaid's Tale*), it is more useful to limit this overview to works that were explicitly redacted as midrashic literature. That is, we shall ignore the numerous works that bear evidence of the midrashic process (such as the birth narratives in the Gospel of Matthew) and focus instead upon those works that Jews traditionally study under the heading of Midrash.[2]

These works consist of homilies and exegetical comments organized in a variety of ways. Primarily they are arranged around the triennial Torah-reading cycle in the Palestinian synagogues (this applies especially to works that comment on the weekly pentateuchal lessons) or they follow an individual book of the Bible verse by verse. It is in this latter category that Midrash Mishle (henceforth MM) falls. There are also other redactive schemes, such as reviews of biblical history (for example, Pirke R. Eliezer or the Targums), topical comments (such as Seder Eliyahu Rabbah), or even commentaries on nonbiblical works (such as Abot de-R. Nathan). Most students of midrashic literature would include here also the many talmudic legends as parts of the corpus of midrashic literature.

Those works concerned primarily with verse by verse commentary are called exegetical Midrashim. Those that comment upon the pentateuchal lessons of special Sabbaths and holy days and thus preserve synagogal sermons—although in a redacted form—are called homiletic Midrashim. These distinctions, however, ignore the fact that the ancient redactors did not classify the midrashic literature quite so tidily; hence full-blown homilies may be found in exegetical Midrashim and word by word exegetical comments may be found in the homiletic Midrashim. In short, works that are entitled Midrash are extraordinarily difficult to categorize, and the boundaries of the genre are disturbingly vague. Still, one may safely date the beginnings of midrashic literature after the destruction of the Second Temple in 70 C.E., when the rabbinic movement as such arose. The closing date for this literature is more indefinite, because Midrash gives way only gradually to commentary as the primary expression of rabbinic exegesis. The rise of Islam and of the Karaite sect brought about an enhanced rabbinic appreciation of the importance of biblical studies. Matters that had generally been ignored in earlier times were now given attention. There suddenly was a new and deep awareness of the nuances of grammar, word meaning, and context.

That awareness marks the clearest distinction between Midrash and medieval Jewish commentary. Whether explicit or implicit, the point of any commentary is the meaning of a verse within its context. Even when quoting earlier legendary comments that have little to do with the plain sense of the biblical text, the commentary tries to make some logical sense out of a verse within its context. That is emphatically not the case in the midrashic process, and this feature distinguishes the two types of literature from each other. Midrash atomizes scriptural verses and tears them out of context. The biblical text is but a vehicle for the transmission of rabbinic concepts. Not only verses but also individual words and even letters can be made the subject of midrashic exegesis, without regard for the context in which they appear in the Bible. Midrash places the scriptural text in a vacuum: commentary places it within a context.

THE PLACE OF MIDRASH MISHLE IN MIDRASHIC LITERATURE

Midrash Mishle marks a watershed in the historic development of midrashic literature, for it stands at the point where Midrash gave way to commentary.[3] MM regularly pays attention to context, going so far as to direct the reader explicitly to note the relation of a particular verse to the verse that precedes or follows it.⁴ This concern, coupled with the often terse comments on the apparent simple meanings of verses, approaches the method of the Karaite Bible commentator Daniel al-Qumisi. MM deals also with the meaning of specific terms in the biblical text, a philological concern that likewise occupied the Arab commentators on the Koran.

Although MM resembles a commentary in its approach to context and philology, it resembles the older midrashic literature in its exegetical comments and its narrative legends. Much of the running comment on the verses of the book of Proverbs employs the methods associated with classical Midrash. The employment of standard hermeneutic norms and the sometimes word-for-word citation of earlier interpretations place MM squarely in the line of midrashic tradition. Like many earlier midrashim, MM concentrates its attention on the opening chapters of the biblical book it treats. It grows notably more laconic in later sections of Proverbs and entirely lacks comment on chapters 3 and 18.

The narrative material of MM is rich and original. The opening chapter recounts a fanciful version of the encounter of King Solomon with the Queen of Sheba. The riddles (1 Kings 10:1–3) she is reported to have proposed to him are cited in inventive detail. Elsewhere in the same chapter MM offers its own version of Joseph's encounter with his brothers. Particular to MM are four distinct stories about legendary deaths. R. Aqiba's death in prison and his burial by Elijah is reported in chapter 9. The death of Elisha ben Abuyah and the faithfulness of his disciple R. Meir are recorded in chapter 6. The death of R. Meir's two sons is reported for the first time in rabbinic literature in MM, chapter 31. A unique and moving version of the death of Moses and of the promise of his resurrection may be found in chapter 14. Other traditional narratives from homiletic Midrashim (such as the story of Vespasian and R. Johanan ben Zakkai in chapter 15 and the story of Moses' encounter with Pharaoh in chapter 27) round out MM's collection of aggadic, or narrative, materials.

Like earlier rabbinic sources, MM has its share of allusions to the mystical literature. There are references to God's "Chariot" and "throne chamber" (*merkabah* and *hekalot* in chapters 8 and 10), to the archangel Metatron (chapter 14), to esoteric speculation (*raze Torah*, chapter 14), and to measurements of God's person (*shiʿur qomah*, chapter 10). All of these traditions, however, seem to be literary, and they are distinct from the earlier mystical traditions upon which they drew.

The early mystical works were primarily liturgical and theurgic—the texts were invoked in order to achieve a certain end, be it to ascend to the Godhead, to win at the racetrack, or to repel mosquitoes. But in MM there begins to be a tendency, carried out more thoroughly in later years, to treat these theurgic works as texts to be studied rather than as liturgies to be invoked. The academic nature of the mystical texts alluded to in MM is underscored in a remarkable passage in chapter 10, where an entire rabbinic curriculum is spelled out in detail.

The "*hekalot* curriculum" begins with the study of Torah. MM offers the astonishing judgment that one who studies Torah alone (to the exclusion of later traditions) is handed over to the guards of Gehenna. We will see later that this passage must be taken as part of MM's anti-Karaite polemic; in this light the negativism of this pronouncement is not quite so astonishing. Following Torah study one must study Mishnah, Midrash on the Pentateuch, rabbinic lore (*haggadah*), and Talmud.[5] Having mastered this part of the curriculum, the student may then turn to more esoteric fields: "Chariot" speculations (*merkabah*), the "throne chamber" and the other aspects of the vision of Ezekiel 1, angelology, the mystery of the fiery stream that flows through the heavens (*rigyon*), and finally *shiʿur qomah,* that most extreme form of mystical contemplation of the Divine Person. After studying all of these esoteric aspects of Jewish mysticism, the initiate may finally learn the secrets of creation itself through the study of the function of God's throne during the six days when the world was created. It is primarily this *hekalot* curriculum that over the past decades has made MM the object of study by experts on Jewish mysticism.[6]

Midrash Mishle also merits study for the number of communal customs mentioned in passing throughout the text. Some attention has already been paid to the statement in chapter 8 that "one is obligated to betake himself early to the synagogue and enter it between its two sets of door posts; only then may he stand in prayer." The two doors of the synagogue seem to indicate a Palestinian custom, for they are mentioned in the Palestinian Talmud, while the Babylonian Talmud is not quite sure what to make of them.[7] MM also mentions the curious system of bowing to the synagogal ark and to the Torah scrolls—a practice known to have been current among the Jews of the diaspora in the ninth century.[8]

In Chapter 31, MM refers to the custom of delivering a homily in the synagogue on Sabbath afternoons. This passing mention is the earliest notice of such a sermon being given at that hour, the earlier custom having been to preach on either Friday night or Sabbath morning. That MM relates this custom to R. Meir shows the concern for verisimilitude with which the MM redactor presents his material, as R. Meir's activities and fame as a preacher are widely reported in the earlier literature.

Another synagogal custom concerns the age of religious majority. MM specifically mentions twenty years, as the age that qualifies a young man to lead the community in prayer. This age of maturity, as opposed to the usual age of thirteen, is also known from earlier rabbinic sources and from the Qumran literature, and was current among the Karaites in the ninth century.[9] Apparent areas of dispute between the Karaites and the Rabbanites concern the use of the *mezuzah*, the phylacteries, and the ritual fringes. On two occasions MM points to the importance of these customs (chapters 8 and 10), presumably in opposition to the Karaite tendency to allegorize these biblical commands and so preclude their actual observance.

The frequent mention of Karaites thus far should make it clear that the author of MM took them under serious consideration. Not only is there some, probably unconscious, influence of Karaite exegetical technique upon the redactor of MM, but there is also an apparent agreement with the Karaite community on the age of majority. On the other hand, as we have noted above, there was disagreement between the Rabbanite redactor and his Karaite contemporaries over their interpretation of the commandments regarding *mezuzah*, ritual fringes, and phylacteries. MM's disagreements with Karaite practices goes even further, reflecting the general extent of the disputes between the two communities.

The synagogue was one place where these disagreements were made evident. Here, without speaking a word, the Rabbanites and Karaites made their differences in practice readily apparent, even to those unfamiliar with the details of the polemic. The Rabbanite custom of bowing to the Torah and to the ark, mentioned above, was one such cause of dispute. The Karaite leader Daniel al-Qumisi complains that "there are monuments among the Jews outside of the arks which are in all of the synagogues in the diaspora. They stand before it in order to bow to it and call it an ark (*aron*) . . . for nowadays they bow to the Torah when they take it out of its housing, and they bow to the ark." Elsewhere Daniel counsels, "And if you have a case to place a book in, place the Torah in one of the synagogues but do not stand before it to bow to it."[10] Thus we see that an everyday practice in the synagogue reflects the separation between the two communities.

Another area of disagreement is prayer. Although it had long been the rabbinic custom to pray three times daily—a practice the rabbis traced back to the patriarchs—the Karaites followed their own prayer schedule. They disagreed with the basic format of the Rabbanite service, centered as it was on the nonbiblical prayer called the 'Amidah (or Eighteen Benedictions). This caused the Rabbanites to begin to canonize their originally fluid liturgy. Karaite leaders justified their own order of prayer by exegetical means. In commenting on Psalm 78, Daniel al-Qumisi states, "Thus you know that it is incumbent upon every man to teach his offspring the works of God and it is forbidden to teach anything outside of the Torah of God, as it is written, *He established a*

decree in Jacob, ordained a teaching in Israel (Ps. 78:5). . . . Thus you must
know that Israel should not say, 'We, too, shall walk in the way of our fathers.'
Rather they should walk in the way of Torah.''[11]

Midrash Mishle seems to respond directly to Daniel's exegesis with its own
interpretations of Proverbs 22:28: "*Do not remove the ancient boundary stone
that your ancestors set up* (22:28)—R. Simeon ben Yoḥai said: If you see a
custom which your forefathers had introduced, do not disdain [other MSS:
change] it—for example, Abraham who instituted the morning prayer, Isaac
who instituted the afternoon prayer, or Jacob who instituted the evening prayer.
. . . What does *that your ancestors set up* mean? R. Joḥanan said: They set not
for themselves alone but for all subsequent generations." While Daniel con-
tends that the way of Torah—that is, Karaism—is the way enjoined upon the
Jews, MM responds that the way of tradition—Rabbanism—*is* the way of
Torah!

The polemic was, however, sharper than even the foregoing exchange indicates. As Salo Baron puts it, "The gross anthropomorphisms of a book like
Sheʾur qomah . . . were ready targets for attack by such opponents as . . . Daniel
al-Qumisi in the ninth century"; and again, "the book *Raza rabba* . . . had
been listed among the objectionable mystic writings by the ninth-century Karaite Bible exegete, Daniel al-Qumisi."[12] We have already noted the extent of
mysticism in MM, including the *shiʿur qomah* material which Daniel had
anathematized. MM seems to be well aware of Daniel's objections when, for
example, it comments in chapter 14, "*A numerous people is the glory of a king;
without a nation a ruler [razon] is ruined* (14:28)—[God said:] If they separate
themselves from [the study of] words of Torah, I in turn will separate the Secrets of Torah (*razey torah*) from them."

Midrash Mishle insists that the Secrets of Torah (akin to, or identical with,
Daniel's *Raza Rabba*?) are revealed only through constant devotion to words
of Torah—that is, to the teachings of the Rabbanite sages. The anti-Karaite
polemic also puts into sharper focus the opening items of the *hekalot* curriculum. It is significant that the content of the curriculum includes direct references to chariot speculation, *rigyon* (the fiery river in heaven), *shiʿur qomah*
("How do I stand, from My [toe]nails to the top of My head? What is the
measure of My hand's span? What is the measure of My foot?"), and creation
mysticism. If this were not enough to antagonize a Karaite like Daniel, how
must he have felt when he read the beginning of the curriculum, which relegates
one who "has [knowledge of] Scripture in hand, but none of Mishnah" to the
guards of Gehenna who fling him into hell? It is only when one realizes that
such a person must be a Karaite that the severity of the sentence becomes ap-

parent, indicating the extent of the breach between the two communities at the time when MM was compiled.

STYLE AND REDACTION

The style employed by the redactor of MM is in keeping with the rabbinic conventions of his time. He interprets the biblical book of Proverbs through his rabbinic perspective, although on occasion he explicates the plain meaning of a verse within its context. A singular example of his penchant for rabbanizing the book of Proverbs may be seen in his treatment of Lady Wisdom, a frequent voice in the biblical text. In MM she is virtually always characterized as Torah—the study of rabbinic teachings—without even recourse to a prooftext to buttress this equation. For the author of MM, there is no wisdom other than that of the rabbinic sages.

The redactor freely combines traditional materials with contemporary inventions. In doing so he often invokes the names of ancient sages as authorities, or reports traditions anonymously. Earlier critics of MM accused the redactor of regularly preferring anonymity, sometimes even when citing verbatim a tradition originally ascribed to a named sage. This is all the more surprising since MM warns that "one who quotes another without naming him . . . brings a curse upon the world," whereas "one who properly cites his source brings redemption to the world" (see the text at Prov. 6:19). Happily, the manuscripts of MM used in the critical edition of the text ascribe many sayings to named sages, making it possible to restore these attributions. Hence it is fair to say that MM cites early traditions under their individual authorities more often than not.

At the same time, MM often invents an individual authority for contemporary materials. This type of spurious attribution was fairly common in medieval times, in both Jewish and Christian literature. Since midrashic literature regularly attributes statements to biblical characters, it was but a short step from there to attribution of other statements to rabbinic sages of earlier times. Thus one finds several dialogues between R. Eliezer and R. Joshua recorded only in MM, for the simple reason that they took place only in the imagination of MM's redactor. So also, the lengthy story of R. Meir and the death of his two sons is the invention of our redactor or of one of his contemporaries. One final example of this phenomenon will suffice: as in all Jewish medieval mystical literature, in MM R. Ishmael is repeatedly mentioned as the authority for the otherwise anonymous mystical traditions.

The redactor of MM was liberal in his use of blocks of earlier texts. In such cases he quotes not merely a single tradition under the name of its tradent, but an entire unit of text. Rarely does MM give the source of such borrowed material, and even then only in the vaguest of ways—"It is taught there"—without specification of just where. These borrowings illustrate the number of ways in which earlier traditions can be transmitted in later works. First, there are records of traditions that agree verbatim with the early texts as we have them. Next, there are recognizable traditions in variant versions. These variants may represent versions differing from those presently in our possession, or they may be the result of scribal garbling of the text. On occasion the hand of the redactor is clearly discernible: the earlier text appears to have been contracted, or imaginatively expanded, or combined with other material, or even rewritten to reflect a somewhat different point of view. A good example of the latter phenomenon is the passage in which MM invokes patriarchal authority for the Rabbanite liturgical practice. The tradition that the patriarchs had coined the various prayer services dates back to the Babylonian Talmud (B. Ber 26b), and the redactor of MM refers to Prov. 22:28, *Do not remove the ancient boundary stone that your ancestors set up,* to produce a polemic against any change.

Midrash Mishle regularly employs traditions from both Babylonia and Palestine. The Mishnah, Tosefta, and Mekilta are quoted, as are Genesis Rabbah and Pesikta de-Rab Kahana, among the Palestinian sources. MM also regularly cites the Babylonian Talmud, Abot de-R. Nathan, and the sixth chapter of the tractate Abot, entitled Qinyan Torah. Earlier critics have emphasized that MM does not quote the Palestinian Talmud, but in fact it remains unclear whether or not MM used it. Even if we assume that the redactor did indeed fail to cite the Palestinian Talmud, it remains unclear whether he knew of it or not.[13] Thus what we are left with is a text that happily draws upon both Babylonian and Palestinian traditions, be they talmudic or midrashic. The use of these two traditions, both of which were known to the communities of Babylonia and Palestine by the time MM was redacted, leaves us with an MM text that is rich in earlier materials but cannot be placed in a particular locale on that basis.

TITLE, DATE, AND
PLACE OF ORIGIN

Today, the universally accepted title of the work translated herein is Midrash Mishle ("Midrash on Proverbs"). It was not always so: the earliest reference to it, in the eleventh-century Hebrew dictionary composed by Nathan ben Jeḥiel of Rome, calls it Haggadat Mishle ("Lore of Proverbs"). It is of course conceivable that there was another work entitled Haggadat Mishle that had a great deal in common with MM. It seems, however, more likely that Haggadat

Mishle is nothing but an alternate title for Midrash Mishle, much the same as Haggadat Tehillim is an alternate title for Midrash Tehillim ("Midrash on Psalms"). MM is referred to once as Shoḥer Tob in the liturgical work known as *Maḥzor Vitry,* also of the eleventh century. Although this may indicate a confusion of MM with Midrash Tehillim (called Shoḥer Tob after the opening words of the text), the fact remains that elsewhere in the *Maḥzor Vitry*[14] our work is referred to as Midrash Mishle. Finally, two later printed editions of MM (Prague, 1613, and Zolkiew, 1800) call it (Midrash) Mishle Rabbeta ("The Great Midrash on Proverbs"). There seems to be no basis for the latter title except the confusion of the seventeenth- and nineteenth-century editors.

The claim to the title Midrash Mishle is thus more firmly established and, as the citation in the *Maḥzor Vitry* may show, the current title was already known as early as the eleventh century. A number of thirteenth-century scholars (including Naḥmanides, Eliezer Roqeaḥ, and Mordecai ben Hillel) and many thirteenth-century manuscripts refer to the work as Midrash Mishle, as do the first two printed editions (Constantinople, 1512–1517, and Venice, 1546).[15]

These same early works, *'Aruk* and *Maḥzor Vitry,* by quoting MM by name and by citing from it passages that are found in the manuscripts and printed editions, supply us with the latest possible date of its compilation—the beginning of the eleventh century. This conclusion, combined with the dates of the works that MM itself quotes and those of the works with which it seems to share materials—in the latter case it is not clear who is quoting whom, but they all can be assumed to have a common contemporary source—helps to determine the range of time within which the redactor of MM was working.

Among the works that MM draws upon, two mentioned above, Qinyan Torah and Abot de-R. Nathan, are the most recent. They are difficult to date precisely, but even so conservative a scholar as Judah Goldin assigns them to the seventh or eighth century at the latest.[16] MM seems to share textual traditions with a number of important medieval works, including the midrashic work Seder Eliyahu Rabba (ninth or tenth century), the code of law *Halakot Gedolot* (ninth century), and a responsum of Hai Gaon (late tenth century). It is possible that the liturgical work *Seder Rab Amram* (late ninth century) quotes MM, but the state of its textual transmission is notoriously poor and quotations from MM may have been added to it from the *Maḥzor Vitry* at a later date. In addition to the *Maḥzor Vitry* and the *'Aruk,* one other eleventh century work, Genesis Rabbati, also quotes MM.[17]

Using this survey of the works that quote MM, those that MM in turn quotes, and those with which MM shares textual materials, one may confidently fix the date of compilation of MM somewhere between the late eighth and late tenth centuries. The linguistic traits of MM's Hebrew style might have confirmed this dating, but unfortunately the flatness of the Hebrew does not offer enough evidence to narrow the date much further.

Other factors in the text, however, may offer some assistance in narrowing the date to the middle of the suggested period—that is, to the ninth century. Certainly some of the customs mentioned, such as bowing to the Torah and the ark, seem to belong to the ninth century, and the mystical literature cited and alluded to by MM are very much a part of that period. The subtle shift in the mystical literature from theurgic liturgy to literary work also may be dated to the ninth century. Already in the tenth century Saadiah Gaon thought of the mystical liturgy as a series of texts to be studied. The *shiʿur qomah* and *Hekalot* literature, which shares a common mystical outlook with MM, also belongs to the ninth century.[18] Moreover, as we have seen above, the customs and the mysticism reflected in MM had come under attack by the Karaite leader Daniel al-Qumisi. As MM seems to have engaged in a dialogue with Daniel, it seems logical to date it within his lifespan, somewhere in the latter part of the ninth century.

One final point in favor of a ninth-century dating is the style of MM, discussed above. The shift from exegetical midrashic style to commentary that is represented in MM clearly belongs in this period. Saadiah's (mid-tenth-century) commentaries are already undeniably of the genre of commentary, although care should be taken to point out that the mixture of styles, as in MM, persists into the twelfth century in Midrash Sekel Tob and Midrash Leqaḥ Tob. In short, all of the factors surveyed point to a ninth-century date for the redaction of MM.

The identification of its provenance is somewhat more complex. Again, a variety of methods can be employed, both internal and external. External methods involve surveying the works that quote MM, those quoted by MM, and those with which it shares material. The provenance of these works might point to a specific locale. Even a cursory glance at the works enumerated above, however, shows that MM quotes both Palestinian and Babylonian works; those with which it shares materials are either Babylonian (responsum of Hai Gaon) or Palestinian (Abot de-R. Nathan, Qinyan Torah) and are first quoted, among the sources available to us today, in Babylonian compilations. Of course, by the ninth century the mutual exchange of textual materials between Babylonia and Palestine was so well established that scholars in each country had complete access to the literary traditions of the other. Thus the works cited by MM and the quotations shared by it with other contemporary works offer few clues as to the provenance of MM.

The first works to quote MM are somewhat more useful in this respect.

Three eleventh-century works have been adduced above as knowledgeable of MM's traditions: the ʿAruk, Maḥzor Vitry, and Genesis Rabbati. None of these three are exclusively Babylonian or Palestinian, but they come from locales which draw upon both of these sources of traditions. The ʿAruk was composed in Rome, and its compiler, Nathan ben Jeḥiel, possessed a thorough knowledge of both Babylonian and Palestinian traditions, the latter having been well disseminated throughout Italy. Maḥzor Vitry and Genesis Rabbati stem from what is today French soil, the former from Vitry and the latter from Narbonne. Both these locales in what the Jews called Ashkenaz (central and northern Europe) are known to have had access to Babylonian traditions. Here again, then, while these findings suggest that MM had won a wide circulation within one or two centuries of its compilation, they offer no firm evidence of its provenance.

Internal evidence suggesting the place of MM's composition includes the customs and current events mentioned therein. The unique custom of bowing to the ark was cited by Daniel al-Qumisi as current in the diaspora. It is also mentioned in the minor talmudic tractate Soferim, a work whose provenance is itself still a matter of debate. Another custom mentioned was entering synagogues through two doors, a custom well understood in the Palestinian Talmud but much less so in the Babylonian. Yet before reaching a hasty conclusion of a Palestinian provenance for MM, one must remember that, as stated above, archeological evidence points to two-entranced synagogues in the diaspora as well as in Palestine. Furthermore, a responsum by Hai Gaon—a Babylonian scholar—addressed to Kairouan shows his thorough awareness of both single-entranced and double-entranced synagogues.[19] Thus of all the customs mentioned in MM, only that of bowing to the ark may possibly indicate a provenance in the diaspora.

The mystical literature of the period regrettably is also less than helpful in determining MM's provenance. While it is clear that MM shows an undeniable affinity with medieval Jewish mysticism, such as the hekalot and shiʿur qomah literature, the locale of origin of even these mystical traditions is far from certain. Although these speculations have traditionally been associated with the schools of Palestine, recent research has raised the possibility of a Babylonian provenance for this kind of mysticism. In short, our inability to fix a definite locale for rabbinic traditions and works of the eighth through the tenth centuries is closely paralleled by our inability to determine the relation of these works to the Karaite literature of the same period.

One would think that MM's anti-Karaite polemic and the Rabbanite-karaite controversy in general would provide sufficient evidence for a secure localization of MM's textual traditions, and particularly that the ability to credit origin of a Karaite tradition to a certain Karaite leader (one who localizes in the diaspora at least one custom mentioned by MM) would point to an identifiable locale. In the case of MM, however, we run afoul of geographical certainty, for Daniel al-Qumisi left his native home in Qumis (in northern Persia) and settled in Jerusalem. Indeed, Daniel brought his Karaite followers with him to live in the land of Israel and exhorted others to join him there. His urgings had reverberations among the Rabbanite communities of Palestine and Babylonia. There was, thus, not only a constant and significant traffic of traders, scholars, and students between Babylonia and the land of Israel, but also a stream of diaspora Jews joining those already living in Palestine.

The result of this constant flow back and forth between Palestine and Babylonia is our inability to place definitively any rabbinic work of this period in one locale or another, unless the author is clearly identifiable as a scholar who lived in a particular city of Palestine or the diaspora (as with Hai Gaon, who resided in Pumbedita in Babylonia). All these considerations lead us to the less than satisfactory conclusion that for the present, the precise locale of MM's composition cannot be determined with any assurance. We must resist the temptation to fix MM in a precise locale (such as Southern Italy or Palestine) and must instead be satisfied with an indefinite spot somewhere along the caravan routes linking the ninth-century Rabbanite communities of Babylonia with those in the land of Israel.

THE PRESENT TRANSLATION

The present translation of MM is the first to appear in English. August Wünsche published a German translation of MM in 1885 in Leipzig, in his series *Bibliotheca Rabbinica*. He relied, however, on faulty printed editions of the text and freely interpolated traditions from the midrashic compilation known as *Yalqut Shim'oni* into the MM text. The present translation is based on the Hebrew critical edition of MM I prepared, which was published by the Jewish Theological Seminary (*Midrash Mishle* [New York: Jewish Theological Seminary of America, 1990]). It is the third part of a trilogy of MM studies I have undertaken during the past decade. My doctoral dissertation included the first draft of a critical edition of the Hebrew text, a preliminary translation of, and commentary on, the first ten chapters of MM, and an extensive introduction. The Hebrew critical edition refined the apparatus of variants and provided complete cross-references to the entire text of MM. The present introduction, translation, and notes reflect the latest results of my research and contain some revised views. Scholars and serious students of MM are advised to consult all three parts of the trilogy.

Although this translation reproduces the basic Hebrew text of MM as found in the Vatican manuscript (Ebr. 44,11), I have occasionally adopted variant readings from other manuscripts or from parallels in order to render the fullest sense of the Hebrew original. As in the critical edition of the Hebrew text, my aim in this translation has been to reproduce the original text of MM, insofar as that is possible. Thus the reader will be able to follow the ninth-century redactor's understanding of the book of Proverbs, reading and interpreting it as if through his rabbinic eyes.

In order to make MM as intelligible as possible to the English reader, a great deal of care has been taken to render the Hebrew text into fluent English without slavish dependence upon literal translations of the original Hebrew idiom. This was a difficult task, as rabbinic Hebrew style deserves careful attention, and its flavor should, to some extent, be preserved. I have paid particular attention to the small semantic units that make up the ongoing narrative and discourse. Philological problems of ninth-century Hebrew were kept in mind, and technical terms and idioms were given particular attention.

Leon Nemoy, the editor of the Yale Judaica Series with whom I first had the privilege of working, was very helpful in reviewing my manuscript with the meticulous attention to detail that is his hallmark. Like the many translations that preceded mine in this series, MM has benefited richly from his vast expertise as a translator. Following Dr. Nemoy's retirement, I had the honor of working with Professor Frank Talmage until his untimely death. He reviewed the entire manuscript, and I profited from his expertise as a medievalist. All of Jewish scholarship is diminished by the loss of this great editor. Finally, I have seen the manuscript through the press under the guidance of Professor Sid Leiman. The patience he exercised in carefully reviewing a work that had already passed through the hands of two other editors is deeply appreciated. My gratitude is extended to Susan Lazev, who served as my research assistant for this project and saved me countless hours and errors, and to Rachel Brodie, who read the proofs and prepared the indexes. I am also grateful for the generous support of the Abbell Research and Publication Fund at the Jewish Theological Seminary of America.

Like any midrashic work, MM is replete with formulaic expressions, particularly introductions to biblical prooftexts. The text abounds in phrases like "as it is written," "as you say," and "thus it is said." These terms were translated with a certain degree of consistency, in order not only to assist the reader who may wish to work his or her way through the Hebrew text and English translation simultaneously, but also to emphasize the importance of the prooftext in rabbinic thought and discussion.

God plays a major role in MM, and therefore appears with regularity. Like all pious Jews, the redactor of MM refrained from referring to God by the

Tetragrammaton, and instead used a series of well-known epithets for God's name. Most of these have been translated to capture their particular flavor. But the terms—"the Holy," "the Holy One, Praised be He," "the Omnipresent," and "the Omnipresent, Praised be He"—are abbreviated in the Hebrew text in such a way that the original idiom cannot be recovered. Because each one of these epithets carries a different theological nuance, I have avoided compounding the theological problem by simply translating each of these particular terms as "God." The reader must, then, be careful not to generalize about the terminology for God in MM from this translation.

As in other volumes of the Yale Judaica Series, a variety of conventions have been observed in order to help the reader through the text. Brackets are used for inserted explanatory material not found in the Hebrew text. Parentheses indicate material that is deemed to be an aside in the flow of the textual narrative. Discourse between sages or biblical characters is enclosed within quotation marks. Individual comments and sayings by rabbinic sages, however, are introduced by a colon, with the initial letter of the following word capitalized and without quotation marks. The paragraphing of the English text is meant only to assist the reader, and either follows the rules of English usage (as in the case of dialogue) or is entirely arbitrary. In the latter case, breaks were made in the unbroken flow of the Hebrew manuscript text simply for ease of reading and comprehension.

Special note should be taken of the numerous biblical quotations found in the text. The new Jewish version of the Bible, the 1982 Jewish Publication Society translation, is generally followed. It is the mark of midrashic literature, however, to take liberties with the biblical text—to pun on it, to twist its plain sense, and often to modify the meaning of a word by a change in its vowels, all for the sake of the homily. In those instances where the JPS translation does not convey the modification of the biblical text intended by the ancient homilist, the translation was changed accordingly. Readers will thus stand to benefit from reading this translation of MM with a copy of the JPS translation on hand—only then will they fully appreciate the extent to which MM plays with the text of Scripture.

The reader will find transliterations of the Hebrew words involved in the frequent puns and wordplays bracketed in the text. The notes include explanations of the devices employed in the exegetical interpretation and references to other rabbinic and cognate sources used by the redactor of MM, as well as references to modern scholarly literature. These notes have been kept to a minimum so that Midrash Mishle may as much as possible speak for itself. The scholar and serious student are urged to consult the other two volumes in my MM trilogy for additional references and more extensive commentary.

THE MIDRASH ON PROVERBS

CHAPTER ONE

. . .

The proverbs of Solomon son of David, king of Israel (Prov. 1:1). Rabbi Tan-
ḥum ben Ḥanilai opened:[1] *But where can wisdom be found?* (Job 28:12)—
this refers to Solomon who fasted forty days[2] so that God[3] might give him the
spirit of wisdom and understanding. As he wandered in search of it, God said
to him, *Ask, what shall I grant you?* (1 Kings 3:5). To which he replied, "I
seek neither silver nor gold from You, only wisdom,"[4] as it is said, *Grant, then,
Your servant an understanding mind [to judge Your people, to distinguish between good and bad]* (1 Kings 3:9).

God responded to him, saying, "Since you have asked for neither silver nor
gold but only for wisdom, *wisdom and knowledge are granted to you*" (2 Chr.
1:12).[5]

And not only that, but wisdom precedes Torah, as it is said, *First wisdom,
[then] fear of the Lord* (Ps. 111:10). It is taught in a Mishnah:[6] R. Eleazar ben
Azariah says: If there is no Torah, there is no right conduct [. . . if there is no
wisdom, there is no fear of the Lord]. Since Solomon's wisdom was given precedence, Scripture says, *and Solomon, though he loved the Lord and followed
the practices of his father David . . .* (1 Kings 3:3)—this[7] shows that Solomon's
wisdom was a gift.[8]

Where is the source of understanding? (Job 28:12). Rabbi Simeon ben Yoḥai said: Wisdom and understanding are synonymous terms; where there is
wisdom there is understanding, and where there is understanding there is wisdom.[9] Since Solomon fasted forty days and sought wisdom, God did not deny
him his reward, as it is said, *The Lord endowed Solomon with wisdom and
discernment in great measure, with understanding as vast as the sands on the
sea shore. [Solomon's wisdom was greater than the wisdom of all the Kedemites
and than all the wisdom of the Egyptians]* (1 Kings 5:9–10).[10]

*He was the wisest of all men: [wiser] than Ethan the Ezrahite, and Heman,
Chalkol, and Darda the sons of Mahol. His fame spread among all the surrounding nations* (1 Kings 5:11). *He was the wisest of all men (ha-adam)*—
this refers to Adam, as it is said, *I am brutish, less than a man (ʾadam)* (Prov.

30:2).[11] *Than Ethan the Ezrahite*—this refers to Abraham,[12] as it is said, *Who has roused a victor from the East (mimizraḥ), Summoned him to His service? Has delivered up nations to him, and trodden sovereigns down? He rendered their swords like dust, Their bows like wind-blown straw* (Isa. 41:2). *And Heman*—this refers to Moses, as it is said, *[My servant Moses . . .] is trusted (ne'eman) throughout My household* (Num. 12:7). *Chalkol*—this refers to Joseph, as it is said, *Joseph sustained (wa-yekalkel) his father, and his brothers* (Gen. 47:12). *And Darda*—this refers to the generation (*dor*) of the wilderness, for they had great knowledge (*de'ah*). *The sons of Maḥol*—for God forgave (*maḥal*) them for that sin [of the Golden Calf]. *His fame spread among all the surrounding nations*—R. Ishmael said: This refers to his wisdom, [the reputation of] which spread from one end of the earth to the other.

Another interpretation: *But where can wisdom be found?* (Job 28:12)—this refers to the Queen of Sheba, who heard of Solomon's wisdom.[13] She said, "I'll go see whether or not he is wise." Whence [do we learn] that she had heard of Solomon's wisdom? From the verse, *The queen of Sheba heard of Solomon's fame, through the name of the Lord, and she came to test him with hard questions* (1 Kings 10:1). What are *hard questions*? R. Jeremiah said: Parables.[14]

She asked him, "Are you Solomon, about whom and whose wisdom I have heard?"

He answered, "Yes."

She said, "If I ask you something will you answer me?"

He answered, *For the Lord grants wisdom; Knowledge and discernment are by His decree* (Prov. 2:6).[15]

She said, "Seven leave and nine enter, two pour and one drinks."

He said, "Surely [this means] seven days of menstrual [unfitness] leave, then nine months of pregnancy enter; two breasts pour [forth milk] and the infant drinks."[16]

She said, "You are a great sage,[17] but if I ask you another question will you answer me?"

He replied, *For the Lord grants wisdom* (Prov. 2:6).

She said, "Who is the woman who says to her son, 'Your father is my father, your grandfather is my husband, you are my son and I am your sister?'"[18]

He replied, "Surely [these are the] daughters of Lot, who say to their sons, 'Your father is my father, your grandfather is my husband, you are my son and I am your sister.'"[19]

She gave him yet another test. She brought in boys and girls, all of the same appearance, all of the same height, all clothed the same. Then she said to him, "Distinguish the boys from the girls."

He immediately motioned to his eunuch to fetch some parched grain and nuts, and began passing them out.[20] The boys unashamedly stuffed their tunics full,[21] but the girls, being modest, [only] filled their kerchiefs. He then told the queen, "These are the boys and those are the girls." She said, "My son, you are a great sage!"

Then she gave him one more test. She brought circumcised and uncircumcised men before him, all of the same appearance, all of the same height, all clothed the same. Then she said to him, "Distinguish between the circumcised and the uncircumcised."

He motioned at once to the High Priest to open the Ark of the Covenant. The circumcised among them bowed from the waist, and their faces were filled with the radiance of the Shekinah,[22] while the uncircumcised among them fell on their faces.[23] Solomon said to her, "These are the circumcised and those the uncircumcised."

"How did you know?" she asked.

He explained, "From [the case of] Balaam, for is it not written, *Who beholds visions from the Almighty [prostrate, but with eyes unveiled]* (Num. 24:4)? Had he not fallen, he would not have seen anything."[24]

If you do not want to learn from Balaam, come and learn from [the case of] Job. When his three friends came to comfort him, he said to them, *But I, like you, have a mind. I fall not beneath you* (Job 12:3)—[what he meant is] "I do not fall down like you do."[25]

At that moment the Queen of Sheba said to Solomon, *But I did not believe the reports until I came and saw with my own eyes that not even the half had been told me; your wisdom and wealth surpass the reports I heard. How fortunate are your men, and how fortunate are these your courtiers, who are always in attendance on you and can hear your wisdom. Praised be the Lord your God, who delighted in you and set you on the throne of Israel. It is because of the Lord's everlasting love for Israel that He made you king to administer justice and righteousness* (1 Kings 10:7–9).

It is said of Solomon, *justice and righteousness,* and it is said of David, *justice and righteousness.* Where [is this said about David]? *And David executed justice and righteousness among all his people* (2 Sam. 8:15). And where [is this said about Solomon]?—*He made you king, to administer justice and righteousness* (1 Kings 10:9). Scripture thus is stating that Solomon's wisdom was equal to David's wisdom, and that David's wisdom was equal to Solomon's wisdom.

Another interpretation: *But where can wisdom be found?* (Job 28:12)— this shows that Solomon was searching for it, asking, "Where is wisdom to be found?" R. Eliezer and R. Joshua [disagreed]; R. Eliezer said, "[Wisdom is found] in the head," while R. Joshua said, "[Wisdom is found] in the heart."²⁶ Solomon came to [agree with] the opinion of R. Joshua, [citing the verse,] *You put gladness into my heart* (Ps. 4:8). And what is *gladness* if not wisdom, as it is said, *Get wisdom, my son, and gladden my heart, That I may have what to answer those who taunt me* (Prov. 27:11).²⁷

David also explicated this in the verse, *Fashion a pure heart for me, O God; create in me a steadfast spirit* (Ps. 51:12). Why was wisdom put in the heart? Because all the other members of the body depend on the heart.²⁸

Solomon said, "I will not do as David, my father, had done. Father commenced his wisdom at the beginning of the alphabet and concluded it in the middle of the alphabet."

Where [is the scriptural proof] that David commenced at the beginning of the alphabet? In the verse, *Happy is the man* (Ps. 1:1). And where [is the scriptural proof] that he concluded in the middle of the alphabet? In the verse, *Let all that breathes praise the Lord* (Ps. 150:6).²⁹

I, however, will not do so. Rather, at the outset I will commence in the middle of the alphabet and then conclude at the end of the alphabet." Solomon said [further], "I will commence at the spot where wisdom is placed. And where is wisdom placed? In the heart. And where is the heart placed? In the middle."³⁰

You may thus say that David followed the words of R. Eliezer while Solomon followed the words of R. Joshua.³¹ R. Eliezer said, "in the head," whereas R. Joshua said, "in the heart." Furthermore, the heart is placed in the hand of God, as it is said, *The king's heart is in the hand of the Lord as channeled water; He directs it to whatever He wishes* (Prov. 21:1). Since the heart is in God's hand, wherever He wishes He inclines it. When Solomon observed that wisdom is placed in the heart, he said, "At the place where wisdom is placed, there shall I begin!" Where [is the scriptural proof of this]? In his Wisdom he explicitly states, *The proverbs of Solomon son of David, king of Israel* (Prov. 1:1).³² Does not everyone know he is David's son, since he states his own name, Solomon? Hence you learn that everything he did was meant for David's honor. *King of Israel*—doesn't everyone know that he was king of Israel? Hence you learn that everything he did was for the honor of Israel.

For learning wisdom and discipline; For understanding words of discernment (Prov. 1:2). If [Scripture says] *wisdom*, why [does it also say] *discipline*? And if *discipline* why *wisdom*? Rather, [the meaning is] if a man has wisdom, he learns [moral] discipline; if he has no wisdom, he cannot learn [moral] discipline. Another interpretation: *For learning wisdom and discipline* (*musar*)— if a man has wisdom, words of Torah will be handed down to him (*nimsarin*); if he has no wisdom, words of Torah will not be handed down to him. *For understanding words of discernment* (Prov. 1:2)—a man must have discernment to infer one thing from another.[33]

For acquiring the discipline for success, righteousness, justice, and equity (Prov. 1:3)—R. Joshua ben Levi said: If one merits [the receipt of] Torah, then he must be discerning in each and every matter [found in the Torah].[34] Another interpretation: *For acquiring the discipline for success*—if one merits [receipt of] Torah, he must be just in all his dealings.[35] Another interpretation: *For acquiring the discipline for success*—when a person is appointed as a judge, he must acquire discernment of how to acquit the innocent and convict the guilty.[36] Another interpretation: *For acquiring the discipline for success*—when a person is appointed as a judge, he must acquire discernment of how to be precise [in rendering] the law, so that he would not sin nor cause others[37] to sin; for if he corrupts judgment, he sins and brings others to sin. But if he renders correct judgment,[38] he accomplishes *righteousness, justice, and equity.* Just as a person may walk on the plains[39] without stumbling, so, too, he who renders correct judgment will not sin nor cause others to sin. Another interpretation: *Righteousness, justice, and equity*—just as a man may run on the plains without stumbling, so, too, he who renders correct judgment will not stumble, and on Judgment Day the angels will run to testify in his behalf.[40]

For endowing the simple with shrewdness (Prov. 1:4)—Solomon said: I was simple, and God gave me shrewdness; I was a young man,[41] and God gave me discretion. Another interpretation: *For endowing the simple [with shrewdness]*—from what age onward should one have shrewdness? From the age of twenty and upward. *The young with knowledge and foresight* (Prov. 1:4): How many years is one called a young man? R. Meir said: Until he is twenty-five; R. Aqiba said: Until he is thirty years of age; R. Ishmael said: Neither according to the one [opinion] nor according to the other, rather until one is twenty years old, for [not] until he is twenty and onward are his sins counted against him, as it is said, *Aged twenty years and over* (Num. 1:20).[42] What does *duties of service* (Num. 4:47) mean?[43] Resh Laqish said: *Service* means prayer, as it is said, *Serve the Lord in gladness* (Ps. 100:2), *[Serve the Lord] in awe* (Ps. 2:11). From the time one is fit for service [he is fit to lead in synagogue worship and held accountable for his deeds].

The wise man hearing them, will gain more wisdom (Prov. 1:5)—R. Jeremiah said: If you see a sage working to grow wise in Torah, know he will be provided with additional Torah. If you see a sage working to grow wiser, know that he will add to his wisdom.[44] *The discerning man will learn to be adroit* (Prov. 1:5). If a person comes to discernment of his own accord, and then goes on to learn Torah [from a sage], he attains life in this world and life in the world to come.[45]

For understanding proverb and epigram (Prov. 1:6). *Proverb* refers to the parables in the Torah; *epigram* refers to the Torah itself. Why is it called *epigram (meliṣah)*? Because it saves *(maṣṣelet)* all who study it from the torment of Gehenna in the future world. Another interpretation: Why is it called *epigram (melisah)*? Because everyone who scorns *(mitloṣeṣ)* the words of Torah will have ridicule heaped upon him, as it is said, *At scoffers, he scoffs* (Prov. 3:34). *The words of the wise and their riddles*[46] (Prov. 1:6). When one hears the words of the sages he should bind them to his heart, as it is said, *Bind them over your heart always* (Prov. 6:21). *And their riddles*—R. Meir said: Even the small talk of the sages is as weighty as all of the Torah.[47]

The fear of the Lord is the beginning of knowledge (Prov. 1:7)—R. Zera said: From this [verse] you learn that Solomon did not concur with the wisdom of his father, David,[48] who said, *The beginning of wisdom is fear of the Lord* (Ps. 111:10), while Solomon said, *The fear of the Lord is the beginning of knowledge* (Prov. 1:7). Are wisdom and knowledge of equal weight?

Fools despise (bazu) wisdom and discipline (Prov. 1:7). It is taught in the Mishnah:[49] Anyone who honors Torah, he himself is honored, etc.[50] Another interpretation: *Wisdom and discipline*—if wisdom, why discipline; and if discipline, why wisdom? [Scripture uses both terms to point out] that if one learns words of Torah and assiduously studies them to the best of his ability, he will have achieved both wisdom and discipline. If he fails to do so, both will be despoiled *(mitbozezin)* from him and he will be called a fool. It is taught in the Mishnah: Because he does not toil at [studying] them, in the end he will try to find a chapter and be unable to do so, or [to recall] the beginning of a tractate[51] and be unable to do so, or the opening of a [scriptural] lesson[52] and be unable to do so, even a verse [will be beyond his recall]. Of him Scripture says, *it was all overgrown with thorns* (Prov. 24:31). Furthermore, since he does not toil [at his studies] he will end up declaring unfit that which is ritually fit and declaring fit that which is ritually unfit! Of him Scripture says, *His face was covered with nettles* (Prov. 24:31). On the other hand, if he studies them to the best of his ability they will cause his face to shine and be luminous, as it is said, *And the knowledgeable will be radiant like the bright expanse of sky* (Dan. 12:3). Since Solomon toiled in them to the degree they required, they added wisdom to the wisdom which he already possessed. Therefore he showed foresight in his Wisdom when he declared, *My son, heed the discipline of your father, And do not forsake the instruction of your mother* (Prov. 1:8).

My son, heed the discipline—which you were commanded on Mount Sinai.[53] Another interpretation: *My son, heed the discipline of your father*—make your ears hear what you were commanded on Mount Sinai. Another interpretation: *My son, heed the discipline of your father*—the moral instruction you were given about honoring one's father. Another interpretation: *My son, heed the discipline of your father*—that was transmitted to you at Sinai regarding honoring one's father. *And do not forsake the instruction (torat) of your mother* (Prov. 1:8)—that was taught (*she-horu*) to you at Sinai regarding honoring one's mother. If you do so you will have fulfilled [the commandment of] the Torah regarding honoring [thy] father and mother.

Another interpretation: *My son, heed the discipline of your father*—[this means] every matter in the Torah handed down to you on Mount Sinai directly from the mouth of the Almighty. *And do not forsake the instruction of your mother*—all that was made explicit in the Torah [so that you may rule] on the fitness of what is fit, and on the unfitness of what is unfit, and on the prohibition of what is forbidden, and on the permission of what is permitted.[54] If you do so the words of Torah will be a crown for your head and a necklace[55] for your throat, as it is said, *For they are a graceful wreath upon your head, a necklace about your throat* (Prov. 1:9). So long as you give voice[56] to them, they will be honey and milk, as it is said, *Honey and milk are under your tongue; and the scent of your robes is like the scent of Lebanon* (Song 4:11).

My son, if sinners entice you, do not yield (Prov. 1:10)—R. Simeon ben Yoḥai said: From whom did Solomon learn to speak thus? You must say, from the wisdom of his father, David. What did David say? *Misfortune pursues sinners* (Prov. 13:21).[57] Therefore Solomon, with the foresight of his wisdom said, *My son, if sinners entice you, do not yield* (Prov. 1:10).

Another interpretation: *My son, if sinners entice you, do not yield*—if a man says to you, "So-and-so is rich—let us go and take his money and kill him," do not heed him, for *They plan only evil against me* (Ps. 56:6). Neither consent nor give heed to them, and if you do [follow] this [advice], you will find that you have fulfilled all of the commandments of the Torah, whereas if you do not, you will find that you have transgressed all the commandments of the Torah.[58] Why? Because anyone who saves a single life in Israel is as though he had saved the entire world; and anyone who destroys a single life is as though he had destroyed the entire world.[59] Not only that, but his sin is also stored up for the future world. Where [is the scriptural proof that] this is so? In that which Scripture goes on to say, *If they say, "Come with us, let us set an ambush to shed blood, let us lie in wait for the innocent without cause"* (Prov. 1:11).[60]

Another interpretation: *Let us lie in wait (niṣpenah) for the innocent without cause*—refers to Joseph's brothers who were looking (*meṣappin*) [for an opportunity] and saying, "When will the time come that we may kill him?" When he came to them they began saying to one another, "This is the day, this is the hour, this is the time!" And the Shekinah laughed at them saying, "Woe unto you for the blood of this righteous man!"[61] Therefore it is said, *Let us lie in wait for the innocent without cause.*[62] Of all of them, Reuben alone wished to save him, as it is said, *But when Reuben heard it, he tried to save him from them* (Gen. 37:21). He said to them, "Come now, I'll give you a piece of advice."

They asked him, "What advice would you give us?"

He said to them, "Let us throw him into the pit alive, *but let us not do away with him ourselves*" (Gen. 37:27).[63] Whence [do we know] that this was so? From what Scripture goes on to say: *Like Sheol, let us swallow them alive, Whole, like those who go down into the Pit* (Prov. 1:12). *Let us swallow them alive*—this refers to Joseph, who descended into the pit alive. *Whole, like those who go down into the Pit*—for he descended in his innocence into the pit,[64] unaware of what they were doing to him. R. Zabdai ben Levi said: Who among all his brothers [actually] let him down into the pit? You must say, Simeon and Levi, as it is said, *Let not my person be included in their council* (Gen. 49:6).[65] But it was Reuben's intention to save him and restore him to his father, as it is said, *Reuben returned to the pit* (Gen. 37:29).

R. Judah and R. Neḥemiah [disagreed].[66] R. Judah said: [Reuben was not at the pit when Joseph was sold because] the burdens of the household had been thrust upon him.[67] After he had discharged his household responsibilities he went over and peeked into the pit, *and saw that Joseph was not in the pit, he rent his clothes* (Gen. 37:29).

R. Neḥemiah said: He was occupied with his sackcloth and fasting,[68] and after he had taken leave of his sackcloth and fasting he went over and peeked into the pit, *and saw that Joseph was not in the pit, he rent his clothes.*

Not only this, but also after they had sold Joseph, the Shekinah laughed at them, saying, *For My plans are not your plans* (Isa. 55:8)—not what you are thinking of—*nor are My ways your ways* (ibid.)—not the way you are speaking—but, *declares the Lord* (ibid.), were it not for the fact that I have so decreed, your counsel would have been for naught.[69]

We shall find every precious treasure, We shall fill our homes with loot (Prov. 1:13). *We shall find every precious treasure*—this refers to the sale of Joseph, for they sold a son who was precious to his father. *We shall find*—he was found to be a lifesaver before them [by saving them from the famine in Canaan]. *We shall fill our homes with loot*—they filled their homes with silver and gold out of Joseph's treasuries.[70]

R. Joshua ben Levi said: The ten martyrs were seized [and slain] just for the sin of selling Joseph. R. Abun said: You must conclude that ten [are martyred] in each and every generation, and still this sin remains unexpiated.[71]

Throw in your lot with us; we shall all have a common purse (Prov. 1:14): *Throw in your lot with us*—when they sat down to dine, he took the chalice[72] and struck it, saying, "Reuben, Simeon, Levi, Judah, Issachar, and Zebulun, the sons of the same mother, come and be seated; Dan and Naphtali, the sons of the same mother, come and be seated; Gad and Asher, the sons of the same mother, come and be seated." Then he struck the chalice again and said, "Benjamin is an orphan [and I too am an orphan].[73] It is fitting for an orphan to sit with an orphan."

We shall all have a common purse—they all shared the same table at the banquet.[74] What did Joseph do? He served each one of them one portion but gave Benjamin five portions. How so? He combined Benjamin's portion, Joseph's portion, Ephraim's portion, Manasseh's portion, and the portion of Asenath, Joseph's wife. And [the scriptural proof that] this was so? *Portions were served them from his table; but Benjamin's portion was five times that of anyone else. And they drank, and were merry with him* (Gen. 43:34).

R. Malai said, quoting R. Isaac of Migdol: From the day when Joseph was separated from his brothers, he did not taste wine, as it is said, *On the brow of the Nazarite because of his brothers* (Gen. 49:26).[75] R. Jose ben Ḥanina said: Neither did they taste wine, as it is said, *And they drank, and were merry with him* (Gen. 43:34)—[only when they were] with him did they drink, [only] with him were they merry.

Another interpretation: *Throw in your lot with us* (Prov. 1:14)—this refers to the Torah which was God's lot, and God gave it to Israel. *We shall all have a common purse*—refers to the moment at Mount Sinai when the Israelites said, *All that the Lord has spoken we will faithfully do* (Exod. 24:7).

My son, do not set out with them, keep your feet from their path (Prov. 1:15). *My son, do not set out with them*—*them* refers to the nations of the world, as it is said, *You shall not set out in the practices of the nation which I am driving out before you* (Lev. 20:23). *Keep your feet from their path*—from worshiping their idols, as it is said, *For you must not worship any other god* (Exod. 34:14). Why so? *For their feet run to evil, They hurry to shed blood* (Prov. 1:16). *For their feet run to evil*—that is idol worship. *They hurry to shed blood*—this shows that [Scripture] considers anyone who worships idols as one who spills blood.

In the eyes of every winged creature the outspread net means nothing (Prov. 1:17): Of whom did Solomon speak in this verse? He spoke of the miserly.[76] R. Joshua ben Levi said: Even birds in the air recognize the miserly and do not enter their nets,[77] hence it is said, *in the eyes of every winged creature. But they lie in ambush for their own blood*[78] (Prov. 1:18)—this refers to the miserly.

They lie in wait for their own lives (ibid.)—this refers to those who have an evil tongue.[79] Who caused them [to be so]? They caused it themselves. And not just for themselves [personally], but also for all that they own, as it is said,

Such is the fate of all who pursue unjust gain; it takes the life of its possessor
(Prov. 1:19). This is what caused [their downfall], as it is said, *Whomever God
delivers into their hand* (Job 12:6).

Another interpretation: *Such is the fate of all who pursue unjust gain* (Prov.
1:19)—this refers to those who take bribes. A parable: A person took a hook
and cast it into the sea. A large fish saw it and, thinking that it was some kind
of food, swallowed it and was caught. Had [the fish] realized [that something
was wrong] it would not have lost its life. So also any person who takes bribes
winds up empty-handed and forfeits his life. Hence it is said, *It takes the life
of its possessor* (ibid.). R. Joḥanan said:[80] If anyone steals [as little as] the value
of a penny from another, it is as though he had taken his life, as it is said, *Such
is the fate of all who pursue unjust gain; it takes the life of its possessor.*

Wisdom cries aloud in the streets (Prov. 1:20): When a sage is sitting and
studying Torah everyone sings his praises, saying, "Happy is this one, for he
has earned wisdom!" *She raises her voice in the square* (ibid.)—this refers to
the disciples of the sages who sit decorously in synagogues and academies and
raise their voices in words of Torah. *At the head of the busy streets (homiyyot)
she calls; at the entrance of the gates, in the city, she speaks out* (Prov. 1:21).
Just as the sea swells (*homeh*) with its waves, so too, when a sage is sitting and
explicating words of Torah, they well up (*homin*) from his heart.[81] Not only
that, but his voice is sweet to God, as it is said, *For your voice is sweet, and
your face is comely* (Song 2:14).

At the entrance of the gates, in the city, she speaks out (Prov. 1:21): When
a sage sits in the gateway of the city or the gateway of the province and studies
words of Torah, he is not embarrassed by passers-by nor even by royalty, as it
is said, *I will speak of Your decrees, and not be ashamed in the presence of
kings* (Ps. 119:46). Another interpretation: *She speaks out* (Prov. 1:21)—when
a man comes before the sage for judgment, he pronounces the guilty guilty and
the innocent innocent, whether he be poor or rich.[82]

*How long will you simple ones love simplicity, You scoffers be eager to
scoff?* (Prov. 1:22): These are the generation of the wilderness. *You dullards
hate knowledge?* (ibid.)—this refers to the evil kingdom that did not accept
Torah. *You are indifferent to my rebuke* (Prov. 1:23)—this refers to Israel,
whom Moses reproved about the incident of the [golden] calf. *I will now speak
my mind to you* (ibid.)—when He promulgated Deuteronomy to them.[83] *And
let you know my thoughts* (ibid.)—this shows that God made known the subtle
points and exegeses of Torah: [ritual] unfitness and fitness, prohibition and
permission.[84]

*Since you have refused me when I called, And paid no heed when I extended
my hand* (Prov. 1:24): *Since you refused me when I called*—this refers to God,

who made His voice audible to Israel,[85] but they continued to sin against Him, as it is said, *How long will you men refuse to obey My commandments and My teachings* (Exod. 16:28)? Another interpretation: *Since you refused me when I called* (Prov. 1:24)—this refers to Moses, who read words of Torah to them but they refused (*meʾanu*) [to listen to] him, as it is said, *How long will they have no faith (yaʾaminu) in Me?* (Num. 14:11). Another interpretation: *Since you refused me when I called* (Prov. 1:24)—this refers to Jeremiah, who called to Israel in Jerusalem to repent, as it is said, *But they refused to pay heed. They presented a balky back* (Zech. 7:11).[86]

And paid no heed when I extended my hand (Prov. 1:24)—this refers to [the angel] Gabriel, for his hand was against Jerusalem for three and a half years.[87] He had live coals in his hand to cast upon Jerusalem, yet he cast them not, for he said, "They would attend to words of Torah." But they did not attend. Another interpretation: *And paid no heed when I extended my hand*— this refers to God, who for many years stretched out His hand [admonishing them] to repent, but they did not repent. Until when [will God continue admonishing them]? R. Jeremiah said, Until God's wrath is [finally] turned away from Israel, as it is said, *I will heal their affliction, Generously will I take them back in love, until[88] My anger has turned away from them* (Hos. 14:5).

You have spurned all my advice, and would not hear my rebuke (Prov. 1:25): *You have spurned all my advice*—this refers to Moses who used to advise the Tribes, but they would disregard his advice behind his back. *And would not hear my rebuke*—this refers to Jeremiah, for they used to spurn and mock him for each and every reproof which he administered to Israel. Jeremiah said to them, "By your lives, the day [of reckoning] will come! Just as you mock and make fun of me [today], some day in the future I will mock and make fun of you!"[89] Where [is the scriptural proof]? From what follows: *I will laugh at your calamity, And mock when terror comes upon you, When terror comes like a disaster, and calamity arrives like a whirlwind; When trouble and distress come upon you. Then they shall call me but I will not answer; they shall seek me but not find me* (Prov. 1:26–28).

Why [will] all of this [occur]? R. Ishmael said: God said to Israel: I told you through My prophet, *Seek the Lord while He can be found* (Isa. 55:6). By your lives! The day will come when you will call Me, and I will not answer you; hence, *Then they shall call me but I will not answer* (Prov. 1:28). Why so? *Because they hated knowledge, and did not choose fear of the Lord; They refused my advice* (Prov. 1:29–30). God said: I told you through My prophet, *Turn back from your evil ways* (Ezek. 33:11). By your lives! The day will come when I will repay you for your ways, as it is said, *They shall eat of the fruit of their ways, and have their fill of their own counsels* (Prov. 1:31). Why so? *The tranquillity of the simple will kill them, and the complacency of dullards will destroy them* (Prov. 1:32). But all who hearken to the words of My Torah shall I settle in quietude and security, as it is said, *But who so listens to me will dwell securely, untroubled by the terror of misfortune* (Prov. 1:33).

CHAPTER TWO

. . .

My son, if you accept my words (Prov. 2:1)—on Mount Sinai God said: My children, if you succeed in accepting My Torah and doing [what is in] it, I will save you from three punishments: the war of Gog and Magog, the pangs of the Messiah['s advent], and the torment of Gehenna.[1] *And treasure up my commandments* (Prov. 2:1)—if you succeed in storing away words of Torah [in your hearts], I will sate you with the stored-up goodness which I have laid away for the future, as it is said, *How abundant is the goodness that You have in store for those that fear You* (Ps. 31:20). God said: In the future I will make known to all the nations of the world that goodness with which I will benefit you, on the condition that your ears listen to the words of Torah, as it is said, *If you make your ear attentive to wisdom, and your mind open to discernment* (Prov. 2:2). How so? *If you call to understanding, and cry aloud for discernment* (Prov. 2:3).

If you seek it as you do silver, and search for it as for treasures (Prov. 2:4)— R. Simeon ben Laqish said: If a man does not go and seek the words of Torah, they will not seek him. Let me tell you a parable: To what may this be likened? To a man who has business affairs—if he does not go after them, they will not go after him. It is taught in a Mishnah: R. Nehoraʾi says: Wander afar to a place of Torah; say not, "It will follow me."[2] Therefore Scripture says, *If you seek it as you do silver, and search for it as for treasures* (Prov. 2:4)—this refers to words of Torah which must be searched for as deeply as the depth of the abyss. Therefore, if a man searches them out, he thereby attains wisdom and understanding, as it is said, *Then you will understand the fear of the Lord, and attain knowledge of God* (Prov. 2:5). If one runs after words of Torah he will find them [right] before him—that is what is [meant when Scripture] says, *And attain knowledge of God* (Prov. 2:5). R. Jeremiah said: Has it not already been said, *[He] gives it to whom He wishes* (Dan. 4:22)? If one longs [to master] words of Torah, God grants them to him, as it is said, *For the Lord grants wisdom* (Prov. 2:6).

Another interpretation: *For the Lord grants wisdom*—by adding wisdom

29

to the wise, as it is said, *He gives the wise their wisdom and knowledge to those who know* (Dan. 2:21). *Knowledge and discernment are by His decree* (Prov. 2:6)—in that He gives speech to the mute, as it is said, *And the Lord said to him, "Who gives man speech?"* (Exod. 4:11)—Scripture does not answer this question by saying "Is it not I, Moses?" but rather by *Is it not I, the Lord* (ibid.)?

Another interpretation: *Knowledge and discernment are by His decree* (Prov. 2:6). God said, *If you produce what is noble out of the worthless, you shall be as My mouth* (Jer. 15:19)—as the mouth which blew a soul into Adam. R. Meir inferred from *If you produce what is noble out of the worthless* that anyone who can bring forth words of Torah from the mouth of the worthless [person] should be considered as worthy as the [divine] Mouth which gives knowledge and discernment.[3]

He reserves sound wisdom for the upright, He is a shield for those that live blamelessly (Prov. 2:7)—R. Eliezer asked R. Joshua,[4] "What is [the meaning of] this verse?"

R. Joshua replied, "My son, from the time a person is formed in his mother's womb, the Torah which he is to learn is reserved for him,[5] and that is why Scripture says, *He reserves sound wisdom*[6] *for the upright, He is a shield for those that live blamelessly*—just as the shield protects a person, so Torah shields all who study it, and that is why Scripture says, *He is a shield for those that live blamelessly*" (Prov. 2:7).

Guarding the paths of justice (Prov. 2:8): If one has been appointed to render judgment, he must *guard the paths of justice and protect the way of those loyal to Him* (ibid.). If he has done so, his ways are preserved from descending into the depths of Gehenna. Hence the sages said: Every one who sits in judgment becomes subject to two things, and these are they: a sword above him, and Gehenna below him. If he renders true justice, he is saved from both; if not, he is handed over to them. *You will then understand what is right, just and equitable—every good course* (Prov. 2:9)—for since he sits in judgment he must understand how to vindicate the innocent and convict the guilty. If he does so, the words of Torah will become plain[7] to him. Not only that, but he also acquires a good portion in this world and a good portion in the world to come, as it is said, *Every good course.* Another interpretation: *Every good course*—since the words of Torah become like a plain road before him, he will not stumble over them. Another interpretation: *Every good course—good refers to Torah,*[8] as it is said, *For I give you good instruction, do not forsake my Torah* (Prov. 4:2). If one forsakes words of Torah, they will forsake him; but if he guards them, they will protect him.

For wisdom will enter your mind (Prov. 2:10). If you acquire words of wisdom, they will give you joy. *And knowledge will delight you* (ibid.)—they will give delight to your mind, as it is said, "If you toil in Torah, I have much reward to give you. But if you neglect Torah, many neglected things will come up against you."[9] *Foresight will protect you and discernment will guard you (tinṣereka)* (Prov. 2:11). If you place your neck (*ten ṣawwarekha*) under the yoke of Torah, it will guard you, as it is said, *When you walk, it will lead you; when you lie down it will watch over you; and when you are awake it will talk with you* (Prov. 6:22). *When you walk it will lead you*—in this world. *When you lie down it will watch over you*—at the moment of death. *And when you are awake it will talk with you*—in the future.[10]

It will save you from the way of evil men, from men who speak duplicity (Prov. 2:12): If you study the words of Torah, they will with great might save you from the way of evil. Why so? Because they resemble a double-edged sword, as it is said, *With paeans to God in their throats and two-edged swords in their hands* (Ps. 149:6). R. Judah, R. Neḥemiah, and the sages [disagreed]: R. Judah said, "*Two-edged*—like a sword which cuts both ways"; R. Neḥemiah said, "*Two-edged*—this refers to the Written Torah and the Oral Torah"; The sages said, "*Two-edged*—for [the Ten Commandments] were written on both sides [of the tablets].[11] So too Torah has laws before it and laws after it." Where [is the scriptural proof for] "before it"? *There He made for them a fixed rule* (Exod. 15:25). And where [is the proof for] "after it"? *These are the rules* (Exod. 21:1).[12]

From men who speak duplicity (Prov. 2:12): this refers to the evil Pharaoh. When Moses came to see him he spoke frowardly. How so? While the sentence was being decreed [against Egypt], Pharaoh would say to Moses, "Go forth and annul the sentence against me, and I will release Israel." So Moses would go forth and request mercy [for Pharaoh and the Egyptians] until [God] would annul the sentence. As soon as Pharaoh saw that the sentence was annulled, he would go back on his word and say to Moses, *I do not know the Lord* (Exod. 5:2). Thus Scripture says, *[It will save you . . .] from men who speak duplicity* (Prov. 2:12).[13]

CHAPTER FOUR

. . .

More than all you guard, guard your mind, For it is the source of life (Prov. 4:23): *More than all you guard, guard your mind*—so that you do not fear the words of Torah. Why? *For it is the source (toṣeʾot) of life.* Hence you learn that life flows (yoṣʾeot) to all the world out of the words of Torah. *Put crooked speech away from you; keep devious talk far from you* (Prov. 4:24): *Put crooked speech away from you*—this refers to an evil tongue, [the effect of] which is as harmful as spilling blood.[1] *Keep devious talk far from you*—that you do not speak to your fellow in one way with your mouth and in another with your heart.

Let your eyes look forward, your gaze be straight ahead (Prov. 4:25): When you stand in prayer, direct both your eyes and your heart toward your Father in heaven; if you do so, *your gaze [will be] straight ahead. Survey the course you take, and all your ways will prosper* (Prov. 4:26): *Survey the course you take*—when you walk to the house of study. If you do so, *all your ways will prosper.*

Do not swerve to the right or the left; keep your feet from evil (Prov. 4:27)—R. Jose the Galilean said: Beware of straying from the words of Torah, neither to the right nor to the left. *Keep your feet from evil*—from the way of evildoers. Another interpretation: *Do not swerve to the right or the left*—R. Krospi said: Beware of straying from the words of the sages, neither to the left nor to the right. *Keep your feet from evil*—so that you do not go the way of the adulterers.

CHAPTER FIVE

· · ·

My son, listen to my wisdom; incline your ear to my insight (Prov. 5:1). Listen
to the words of my Torah when you study them. *Incline your ear to my insight*—attend well at the time of the lecture hour. *That you may have foresight
while your lips hold fast to knowledge* (Prov. 5:2)—providing that you have
learned in order to observe and have listened in order to keep [the command-
ments].

*For the lips of a forbidden woman drip honey; her mouth is smoother than
oil* (Prov. 5:3): My son, beware of the promiscuous woman lest she mislead
you with her words.[1] *Her mouth is smoother than oil*—[beware] lest she entice
you after her voice. Why so? *In the end she is bitter as wormwood, sharp as a
two-edged sword* (Prov. 5:4). R. Eliezer asked R. Joshua,[2] "Master, what does
this term *two-edged sword* mean?"[3] He replied, "My son, just as the sword
cuts both ways, so the promiscuous woman destroys a man's life in this world
and in the world to come."

What is written following this? *Her feet go down to Death; her steps take
hold of Sheol* (Prov. 5:5). *Her feet go down to Death*—for she drags man down
in this world to the depths of the shadow of death. And what are the depths
of the shadow of death? They are terrible sufferings. *Her steps take hold of
Sheol*—for although he is condemned to suffering in this world, he is nevertheless not saved from the torments of Gehenna in the future. *She does not
chart a path of life; her course meanders for lack of knowledge* (Prov. 5:6). My
son, do not leave the path of life lest you should stumble. Do not stray after
the way of the harlot. Why so? *Her course meanders for lack of knowledge.*
But if you listen to the words of My Torah and the pronouncements of My
mouth you will never stumble. *So now, children, pay heed to me, and do not
swerve from the words of my mouth* (Prov. 5:7). Rather, *Keep yourself far away
from her; do not come near the doorway of her house* (Prov. 5:8). Why so?
Lest you give up your vigor to others, your years to a ruthless one (Prov. 5:9).

Lest you give up your vigor to others—because she causes the glory[4] of the
Shekinah to be removed from you. *Your years to a ruthless one*—for you will

be handed over to a ruthless angel. *Lest strangers eat their fill of your strength, and your toil be for the house of another* (Prov. 5:10): *Lest strangers eat their fill of your strength*—for in the future ruthless angels will take their satisfaction from you in Gehenna.[5] *And your toil be for the house of another*—for you will be considered by them as an Other. Not only that, but you will come to regret it[6] in the end, as it is said, *And in the end you roar when your flesh and body are consumed, and say, "O how I hated discipline, and heartily spurned rebuke. I did not pay heed to my teachers or incline my ear to my instructors. Soon I was in trouble amidst the assembled congregation"* (Prov. 5:11–14). What caused you [to come to this pass]? The evil environment in which you grew up.

Drink water from your own cistern, running water from your own well (Prov. 5:15). How so? If one wishes to study Torah he should not say, "I will study [first] with the [teacher who is] far away and [only] thereafter with the [teacher who is] nearby"; rather study [first] with the [teacher who is] nearby and thereafter with the [teacher who is] far away. *Your springs will gush forth in streams in the public squares* (Prov. 5:16)—R. Eleazar said: If you see a generation to whom the words of Torah are dear, *let your springs gush forth;* if not, *let them be yours alone, others having no part with you* (Prov. 5:17). *Let your fountain be blessed* (Prov. 5:18)—hence the sages have said: Happy is the man whose wife is from his native city, his Torah is from his native city, and his livelihood is in his native city. Of him [Scripture] says, *Let your fountain[7] be blessed; find joy in the wife of your youth* (Prov. 5:18).

R. Samuel bar Naḥmani said: Happy is he who has acquired Torah in his youth, as it is said, *Find joy in the wife of your youth* (Prov. 5:18). [Where in Scripture do we learn] that this phrase refers to Torah? From what follows this verse: *A loving doe, a graceful mountain goat. Let her breasts satisfy you at all times; be infatuated with love of her always* (Prov. 5:19).[8]

Why be infatuated (tishgeh), my son, with a forbidden woman? Why clasp the bosom of an alien woman (Prov. 5:20)? It is better for you to attend (*tashgiah*) to the words of Torah which lengthen the days of man than to *clasp the bosom of an alien woman;* it is better to embrace the bosom of Torah[9] which causes you to earn merit than to *embrace the bosom of an alien* who causes you to sin. *For a man's ways are before the eyes of God; He surveys his entire course* (Prov. 5:21): One should not say, "I will go and sin, for God will not see me."[10] Why [might one think that God will not see him]? *For God is in heaven, and you are on earth* (cf. Eccles. 5:1). Notwithstanding this [verse], you must know that *a man's ways are before the eyes of God* (Prov. 5:21).

Another interpretation: *For a man's ways are before the eyes of God* (Prov. 5:21)—if one sets out on the way to [perform] a commandment, that commandment is accounted to him [as performed, whether he gets to it or not]. If one sets out on the way to [commit] a sin, that sin is accounted to him [as committed, whether it is so or not].[11] *He surveys his entire course* (Prov. 5:21)—hence the sages have said:[12] Know that there is above you a seeing eye and a hearing ear, and all your deeds are written down in a book.

The wicked man will be trapped in his iniquities; he will be caught up in the ropes of his sin (Prov. 5:22): Just as a man spreads out a net and catches fish out of the sea, so does God spread a net to entrap the sinner; therefore it is said, *The wicked man will be trapped in his iniquities; he will be caught up in the ropes of his sin.* Just as a woman's iniquities are recalled to her only during her labor pains,[13] so a man's iniquities are recalled to him only when he comes to the pains of the nether world;[14] hence it is said, *He will be caught up in the ropes of his sin.*

He will die for lack of discipline, infatuated by his great folly (Prov. 5:23): *He will die for lack of (en) discipline*—he will die in his iniquity (ʿawon) because he did not heed moral discipline. *Infatuated (yishgeh) by his great folly*—he did not wish to dote on (yisgeh) moral discipline, so now *infatuated by his great folly [he shall reel].*

CHAPTER SIX

. . .

My son, if you have stood surety (ʿaravta) for your fellow, given your hand for another (zar) (Prov. 6:1): My son, if you have become entangled (ʿeravta) [sexually] with your neighbor, with the seed (zerʿ) of your companion, you have given your hand to [the] strangeness [which is idolatry].[1] Just as [the participant in] idolatry is condemned to Gehenna, so will you likewise be condemned to Gehenna. Another interpretation: *My son, if you have stood surety for your neighbor*—this refers to Israel when they stood before Mount Sinai.

God said to them, "If I give you My Torah, will you uphold it?"

They said, "Yes!"

God said to them, "I demand sureties from you."

They said, "We offer you heaven and earth [as sureties]."

He replied, "I do not want anything ephemeral."

Why so? Because they will pass away in the future.[2]

He said further, "I have [in mind] better sureties—your children! If you uphold the words of My Torah, I will preserve your children; if not, I will snatch them away from you," as it is said, *Because seeing you have spurned the teaching of your God, I, in turn will spurn your children* (Hos. 4:6).

At that moment Israel accepted the Torah and gave their children as sureties. Where [in Scripture] are Israel called *My children?* In the verse, *Israel is My child, My firstborn* (Exod. 4:22). Another interpretation: *Israel is My child, My firstborn*—for they lent primogeniture to good deeds[3] [when they stood] before Mount Sinai.

Given your hand for another (Prov. 6:1): If you forget the Torah which I have given you with My right hand, on Judgment Day I will turn cruel against you;[4] hence Scripture says, *Given your hand for another*. Another interpretation: *Given your hand for another*—God said to them: If you are meritorious and uphold My Torah which was given to you by [My] right hand, well and good. If not, on Judgment Day you will be considered strangers by Me; hence Scripture says, *given your hand for a stranger*.

You have been trapped by the words of your mouth, snared by the words of your mouth (Prov. 6:2). In the future God will say to Israel on Judgment Day: Since you have let My Torah be forgotten [and cease issuing] out of your mouths, I shall condemn you. Did you not tell Me, "*All that the Lord has spoken we will faithfully do*" (Exod. 24:7)? Where is all that faithful doing? Hence God will hold them liable in judgment, and that is why Scripture says, *You have been trapped by the words of your mouth, snared by the words of your mouth* (Prov. 6:2)—you failed [to keep] the words of your mouths, you were snared by the words of your mouths. At that moment God will say to them, My children, since you have suffered under foreign dominion,[5] let that [suffering] atone for this [transgression]. Go, therefore, and bring the patriarchs who studied this [Torah], and they will save you from the torment of Gehenna.

Where is [the scriptural proof] that this is so? In the verse, *Do this, then, my son, to extricate yourself, for you have come into the power of your fellow;[6] go, grovel and badger your fellow* (Prov. 6:3). The patriarchs [will] respond to Israel, saying, Since you have been caught by the nets of Judgment Day, all you can do is sit and study Torah, as it is said, *Give your eyes no sleep, your pupils no slumber* (Prov. 6:4)—while studying words of Torah. Why so? Because the [study of] Torah atones for sin.[7]

Another interpretation: *Give your eyes no sleep*—while repenting, for penitence and good deeds act as a shield against retribution.[8] Another interpretation: *Give your eyes no sleep*—while fasting. Why so? Because fasting leads to repentance, as it is said, *Rend your hearts,[9] rather than your garments, and turn back to the Lord your God* (Joel 2:13). If you have done so, *He is gracious and compassionate, slow to anger, abounding in kindness, and renouncing punishment* (ibid.). And why [should one go on] to this extent? In order to be delivered[10] from the torment of Gehenna. This is what Solomon explicates in the Writings,[11] *Save yourself like a deer out of the hand [of a hunter], like a bird out of the hand of a fowler (yaqush)* (Prov. 6:5)—so that you are not smitten (*tinnaqesh*) by the descent into Gehenna. Another interpretation: *Like a bird out of the hand of a fowler (yaqush)*—so that you not become as chaff (*yaqush*) for the fire of Gehenna, seeing that the power of repentance reaches even to the Throne of Glory.[12]

R. Joshua's students asked him, "Master, which is greater, repentance or charity?"

He answered them, "Repentance is greater than charity, for one sometimes gives charity to a person who does not deserve it, whereas repentance is offered by the penitent himself."

They replied, "But master, have we not already found charity [*ṣedaqah*, literally, "righteousness"] to be greater than repentance, since Scripture says regarding Abraham, *[And because he put his trust in the Lord,] He reckoned it to him for righteousness (ṣedaqah)* (Gen. 15:6), and elsewhere it says, *It will therefore be to our righteousness (ṣedaqah)* (Deut. 6:25)? Not only that, but David came and explained it [by saying], *Your righteousness (ṣedaqah) is like the high mountains; Your justice like the great deep; man and beast You deliver, O Lord* (Ps. 36:7)."

Lazybones, go to the ant; study its ways and learn (Prov. 6:6)—R. Judah ben Pedaiah said: In the future the wicked will say to God, "Master of both worlds, allow us to do so, and we will offer penitence before You!"

God will reply to them saying, "O you consummate fools! The world you were [living] in resembles the eve of the Sabbath, whereas this [next] world [of Judgment] is like Sabbath itself. If a person does not prepare [his Sabbath meal] on the eve of the Sabbath, what will he eat on Sabbath day?[13] The world you were [living] in resembles dry land, whereas this world [of Judgment] is like the sea. If a person does not prepare [provisions] on dry land, what will he eat at sea? The world you were [living] in resembles a vestibule, whereas this world [of Judgment] is like a dining chamber.[14] If a person does not arrange himself in the vestibule, how can he enter the dining chamber? The world you were [living] in resembles summer, whereas this world [of Judgment] is like winter.[15] If a person does not plow and plant in summer, what will he eat in winter? Not only this, but should you not have learned [at least] from the ant?" Hence Scripture says, *Lazybones, go to the ant; study its ways and learn* (Prov. 6:6). What is its wisdom? *It lays up its stores during the summer, gathers in its food at the harvest* (Prov. 6:8).

(*Without leaders, officers, or rulers* [Prov. 6:7]—R. Eleazar asked R. Joshua, "Master, what is the meaning of this verse?"

Rabbi Joshua replied, "My son, the ant has neither king, nor overseer, nor ruler to make her wise, rather her wisdom comes from within her.")[16]

[God continued His rebuke, saying:] "And you wicked ones, should you not have learned from her? Yet you held on to your indolence and your foolishness and failed to repent!" Therefore Solomon said, *How long will you lie there, lazybones; When will you wake from your sleep* (Prov. 6:9)?

A bit more sleep, a bit more slumber, a bit more hugging yourself in bed (Prov. 6:10): *A bit more sleep (shenot)*—so that you can arise to your studies (*mishnateka*). *A bit more slumber*—so that you can arise to your prayers.[17] *A bit more hugging in bed*—refers to sexual intercourse.[18]

And poverty will come calling upon you, And want, like a man with a shield (Prov. 6:11): This refers to the King Messiah who will march in the future at the head of Israel, as it is said, *Their king marches before them, the Lord at their head* (Micah 2:13).[19]

A scoundrel, an evil man lives by crooked speech (Prov. 6:12)—these are the evil-tongued [informers] whom God likens to idolaters. Why so? Because informing is as vicious as idolatry. R. Joshua said: [God] likened them rather to murderers, for informing is as vicious as spilling blood. Of murderers it is written, *Whoever sheds the blood of man, By man shall his blood be shed* (Gen. 9:6). So too, here, when [the informer] goes forth and denounces someone to the government, it is the same as if he had spilled his blood. Not only that, but even Solomon in his wisdom spoke of his corruption and cursed him. Where [in Scripture] is his corruption [described]? In the passage, *Winking his eyes, shuffling his feet, pointing his fingers;*[20] *duplicity is in his heart, he plots evil all the time; he incites quarrels* (Prov. 6:13–14). And what follows this? A curse—*Therefore calamity will come upon him without warning; suddenly he will be broken beyond repair* (Prov. 6:15).

Six things the Lord hates; seven are an abomination to Him (Prov. 6:16). These are the six that God hates: *A haughty bearing, a lying tongue, hands that shed innocent blood, a mind that hatches evil plots, feet quick to run to evil, a false witness testifying lies, and one who incites brothers to quarrel* (Prov. 6:17–19).[21] These are the *seven [which] are an abomination to Him:* idol worship, sexual immorality,[22] spilling of blood, an evil tongue,[23] an adulterous elder,[24] one who [obsequiously] flatters another with words,[25] and one who quotes another without naming him and thus brings a curse to the world. Yet one who properly cites his source bring redemption to the world, as it is said, *And Esther reported it to the king in Mordecai's name* (Est. 2:22).[26]

My son, keep your father's commandment; do not forsake your mother's teaching (Prov. 6:20). What follows this? *Tie them over your heart always; bind them around your throat* (Prov. 6:21). Why so? Because *When you walk it will lead you* (Prov. 6:22)—in this world. *When you lie down, it will watch over you* (ibid.)—at the moment of death. *And when you are awake it will talk with you* (ibid.)—in the coming future.[27]

It is taught there:[28] Rabbi [Judah, the Patriarch] says: Make a lamp for yourself that you may walk by its light. What [light] is this? It is the light of Torah, as it is said, *For the commandment is a lamp and the Torah is a light, and the way to life is the rebuke that disciplines* (Prov. 6:23). Hence R. [Meir][29] said: Happy is the person who has acquired Torah in his youth! Why so? Because Torah preserves him from [taking] the evil way and [from] all those who have too much knowledge, as it is said, *It will keep you from an evil woman, from the smooth tongue of a forbidden woman* (Prov. 6:24).[30] Beware of her so that her beauty may not lead you astray, as it is said, *Do not lust for her beauty* (Prov. 6:25). What follows this? *The last loaf of bread will go for a harlot; a married woman will snare a precious person* (Prov. 6:26).

R. Meir asked Elisha ben Abuyah, his teacher,[31] "Master, what [is the meaning of], *A married woman will snare a precious person?*"

Elisha replied, "My son, if an unlearned man is caught in sin, it is no disgrace for him. Why so? Because he can say, 'I am but an unlearned man—I did not know the punishment [prescribed] in the Torah!' But if a *ḥaber* is caught in sin, it is a disgrace for him. Why so? Because he mixes purity with impurity. He casts shame upon the Torah which he had held precious and the unlearned are bound to say, 'Come and look at the *ḥaber* who got caught in sin—is this his Torah?'[32] Hence Scripture says, *She snares a precious person.*"

(R. Abbahu said: What [is the meaning of] *snares*? He is trapped in the [hunter's] net. R. Alexandri said: What is [the meaning of] *precious*? This refers to the Torah, as it is said, *She is more precious than rubies; all of your goods cannot equal her* [Prov. 3:15]. Therefore it is said, *She snares the precious person.*)[33]

R. Meir asked Elisha, "Master what is the punishment for adultery in the coming future?"[34]

Elisha replied, "My son, since you ask me about this matter, come and see what is said further on in this subject, *Can a man take embers into his bosom without burning his clothes? . . . It is the same with one who sleeps with his fellow's wife; none who touches her will go unpunished* (Prov. 6:27, 29). It is said here, *will not go unpunished,* and it is said regarding the profanation [of God's name] by the false oath, *[The Lord] will not leave unpunished [one who swears falsely by His name]* (Exod. 20:7). Just as there [the one who swears falsely forfeits] all of his money, so here, *will not go unpunished* [means] he forfeits all his merits."[35]

R. Meir asked, "Master, has he no recourse?"

Elisha answered, "Son, once I sat before my colleague ben Azzai, and we were studying this section of Scripture. When we reached this verse he said to me, 'Let him go forth and raise an orphan in his home[36] and teach him Torah, and instruct him in all the commandments. This will atone for him in the world to come, providing that he changes his ways and repents.'[37] I said to him, 'Master, where is the [scriptural] evidence for this?' He said, 'It is written, *If you return, O Israel, declares the Lord—If you return to Me* (Jer. 4:1). Why? *For I am compassionate—declares the Lord, I do not bear a grudge for all time* (Jer. 3:12).' I told him, my son, that he had a better prooftext, to wit, the verse, *Return, O Israel, to the Lord your God; for you have fallen because of your sin* (Hos. 14:2)—even if you had denied God.[38] If God accepts a penitent who had denied Him, surely He will accept an adulterer when he offers penitence."

His disciple [Meir] responded to him saying, "Master, don't your ears hear what you say? If God accepts the penitence of these, how much more so [will He accept] you who know all of the Torah![39] Why then do you not repent?"

Elisha replied: "Son, once I entered a synagogue and saw a student sitting in front of his teacher who was making him recite Scripture. The teacher recited first,[40] *And to the wicked (we-la-rasha᷅) God said, 'Who are you to recite My laws?'* (Ps. 50:16). Then the student recited it, *And to Elisha (u-le-Elisha᷅)*[41] *God said, 'Who are you to recite My laws, and mouth the terms of My covenant?'* (ibid.). When I heard that, I said, 'The decree [against me] has already been sealed from above.'"[42]

R. Meir then responded, saying, "Master, you repent in this world, and I will take care of your sentence [to be delivered] to the executioner[43] on Judgment Day in the coming future!"

Nevertheless Elisha did not accept [this challenge]. After he died people came and said to R. Meir, "Come look at the fire that is consuming the grave of your teacher." Then R. Meir spread his cloak over the grave of his teacher and adjured the fire, saying, *Stay for the night. Then in the morning, if he will act as a redeemer, good! Let him redeem. But if he does not want to act as a redeemer for you, I will do so myself, as the Lord lives! Lie down until morning* (Ruth 3:13). *Stay for the night*—in this world which is night. *Then in the morning*—in the world to come. *If he will act as a redeemer, good! But if he does not want to act as the redeemer for you, I will do so myself, as the Lord lives!*—once he invoked God's name upon it the fire died down.[44] Hence the sages have said, "Happy is the man that raises disciples who will stand up [to plead for mercy in his behalf]."

A thief is not held in contempt for stealing to satisfy his soul and appease his hunger (Prov. 6:30). If you see an unlearned man who wears himself out [to study] Torah, do not despise him. Say not, "Yesterday unlearned and today a ḥaber!" Why so? [Because he does so] *to satisfy his soul and appease his hunger.* And [in Scripture] hunger can refer only to hunger for Torah, as it is said, *Not a hunger for bread or a thirst for water, but for hearing the words of the Lord* (Amos 8:11). Another interpretation: *A thief is not held in contempt*—if you see a wicked man turning away from his wickedness, do not despise him. Why so? [Because he repented in order] *to satisfy his soul and appease his hunger.*

What is written following this? *Yet if caught he must pay sevenfold; he must give up all the substance of his house* (Prov. 6:31)—this refers to the unlearned man who returns to his former misdeeds after he had learned Torah. God turns him over to the fourteen compartments of Gehenna.[45] It is not enough that he brings this [calamity] upon himself, but he brings it also upon his household and his fortune, as it is said, *He must give up all the substance of his house.* Another interpretation: *Yet if caught he must pay sevenfold*—this refers to the one who studies Torah. If he studies Torah but does not perform [the commandments enjoined therein], God turns him over to the fourteen compartments of Gehenna. It is not enough that he brings this upon himself, but he brings it also upon his fortune, as it is said, *He must give up all the substance of his house.* Another interpretation: *Yet if caught he must pay sevenfold*—this refers to the judge. From the moment he is appointed to public office, if he does not judge fairly and render true justice, God turns him over to the fourteen compartments of Gehenna. It is not enough that he brings this upon himself, but he brings it also upon his fortune, as it is said, *He must give up all the substance of his house.*

He who commits adultery is devoid of sense; only one who would destroy himself does such a thing (Prov. 6:32)—R. Zebidah said: What does [Scripture mean by] saying, *He is devoid of sense; only one who would destroy himself does such a thing?* [It means] that the Omnipresent One removes wisdom from his heart.[46] For [in Scripture] wisdom means Torah, as it is said, *The Torah of the Lord is perfect, renewing life; [the decrees of the Lord are enduring, making the simple wise]* (Ps. 19:8). Moreover, the radiance of his face is dimmed because of this [lack of] wisdom. Where [is the scriptural proof] that a person's radiance [reflects] wisdom? In the verse, *A man's wisdom lights up his face, so that his deep discontent is dissembled* (Eccles. 8:1).[47] Furthermore, the evil reputation of the adulterer is never erased, as it is said, *He will meet with disease and disgrace; His reproach will never be expunged* (Prov. 6:33). When he comes up on Judgment Day, God will not forgive him but will be filled with rage against him.

Let me tell you a parable: To what may this be likened? To a legion that rebelled against the king. What did the king do? He took up his weapons of war and marched forth to engage it. When he arrived at [the legion's camp] he began to smite them unceasingly in his rage, because of the indignation [burning] inside him. Hence it is written, *The fury of a man will be passionate, He will show no pity on his day of vengeance* (Prov: 6:34). So too in the coming future God will be filled with rage against transgressors. That is why Scripture says, *He will show no pity on his day of vengeance.*

What is written following it? *He will not have regard for any ransom; He will refuse your bribe, however great* (Prov. 6:35). R. Abbahu said: This is to teach you that God's way is not like the way of flesh and blood. When flesh and blood is filled with rage toward his fellow, he may be appeased by words. But God is not like that, *He will not have regard for any ransom.* With flesh and blood, if you can not appease him with words, you may appease him with money. But God is not like that, *He will refuse your bribe, however great.* Hence you learn how severe is the punishment for sin. Not only that, but Solomon prophesied about it in his Wisdom,[48]

CHAPTER SEVEN

. . .

Let your mind not wander down her ways, do not stray onto her paths (Prov. 7:25). Why so? *For many are those she has struck dead, and numerous are her victims* (Prov. 7:26). What follows this verse? *Her house is a highway to Sheol leading down to Death's inner chambers* (Prov. 7:27). From this [concatenation of verses] Rabbi [Judah the Patriarch] concluded: Happy is he who keeps his heart far from sin and calls [instead] upon wisdom, for as he calls upon wisdom, he is answered by understanding, as it is said,[1]

CHAPTER EIGHT

. . .

It is Wisdom calling, Understanding raising her voice (Prov. 8:1).[1] Whence will she put forth her voice? R. Levi said: From the highest heights of the universe,[2] as it is said, *She takes her stand at the topmost heights, By the wayside, at the crossroads* (Prov. 8:2). What follows this verse? *Near the gates, at the city entrance; At the entryways she shouts* (Prov. 8:3). No sooner do you call to wisdom than she stands [ready to serve you] at your gates. Therefore it is said, *Near the gates, at the city entrance; At the entryways she shouts.* No sooner do you sit chanting[3] words of Torah than she chants at your doors. Therefore it is said, *At the entryways she shouts.*

Come and see how great is the greatness of the wisdom of Solomon, king of Israel. He cries out in full voice about it, saying, *O men, I call to you; my cry is to all mankind* (Prov. 8:4). If he calls them *men* why does he then call them *mankind?* R. Simeon ben Ḥalfota said: If you have [earned the] merit of upholding the words of Torah, you will be referred to [in the same way] as Abraham, Isaac, and Jacob,[4] who upheld the Torah and were called *men.* If not, you will be called not *men,* but *mankind (adam),* like Adam, who did not uphold the Torah and was banished from the Garden of Eden.[5]

Another interpretation: If you have [earned the] merit of upholding the words of Torah, you will be called *men,* as are the ministering angels.[6] If not, you are [to be called] *mankind.*[7] What follows this verse? *O simple ones, learn shrewdness; O dullards, instruct your minds. Listen, for I speak noble things; right things come from my lips* (Prov. 8:5–6). What is [the meaning of] *noble things (negidim)?* Things which tell you *(maggidim)* [the difference] between fit and unfit, between forbidden and permitted.[8] What is [the meaning of] *Right things come from my lips?* Things which open for you the innermost chamber on high.[9]

My mouth utters truth; wickedness is abhorrent to my lips (Prov. 8:7). When a person sits studying words of Torah, *My mouth utters truth.* But when a person diverts his lips to scoffing [at the Torah], *wickedness is abhorrent to my lips. All my words are just, None of them perverse or crooked* (Prov. 8:8).

This shows you that so long as one studies words of Torah he will never stumble. Why so? Because *All are straightforward to the intelligent man, and right to those who have attained knowledge* (Prov. 8:9).

R. Neḥemiah said: Come and see what a good thing God had created in His world even before He created the universe. What may this be? It is the Torah! It is taught there,[10] that seven things were created before the creation of the universe, and they are these: Torah, the Throne of Glory, the Temple [in Jerusalem], the Garden of Eden, Gehenna, Repentance, and the name of the Messiah. What [is the scriptural proof for] the throne of Glory? The verse, *Your throne stands firm from of old*[11] (Ps. 93:2). What [is the scriptural proof for] the Temple? *O Throne of Glory, exalted from of old, our sacred shrine* (Jer. 17:12). And what [is the scriptural proof for] the Garden of Eden? The verse, *The Lord God planted a garden of old,*[12] *in Eden* (Gen. 2:8). What [is the scriptural proof for] Gehenna? The verse, *The Topheth has long been ready for him . . . with plenty of fire and firewood, And with the breath of the Lord, Burning in it like a stream of sulfur* (Isa. 30:3). What [is the scriptural proof for] Repentance? The verse, *Before the mountains came into being, before You brought forth the earth and the world, from eternity to eternity You are God* (Ps. 90:2). What follows this verse? *You return man to dust; You decreed, "Return, you mortals!"* (Ps. 90:3). What [is the scriptural proof for] the name of the Messiah? The verse, *May his name be eternal; before the sun his name was Yinnon*[13] (Ps. 72:17). What [is the scriptural proof for] Torah? *The Lord created me at the beginning of His course, As the first of His works of old* (Prov. 8:22). What is written just before it?[14] *I endow those who love me with substance,* etc. (Prov. 8:21)—R. Joshua ben Levi said: In the coming future God will bequeath three hundred and ten worlds to each and every righteous person according to the numerical value of *substance (yesh).*[15] Therefore it is said, *I endow those who love me with substance.*

At first Torah was in heaven, as it is said, *I was with Him as a confidant* (Prov. 8:30). Later on Moses arose and brought it down to earth to give it to humanity,[16] as it is said, *Rejoicing in His inhabited world, Finding delight with mankind* (Prov. 8:31). R. Alexandri said: What is [the significance of] *inhabited world?* From this [redundancy] you learn that it is called by ten names: land, earth, dry ground, dry land, ground, world, abode, beginning, valley, field.[17] [It is called] land (*ereṣ*), for people run (*raṣim*) on it; earth (*adamah*), for Adam was created out of it; dry ground (*ḥarabah*), for the [flood] waters lay it waste (*maḥribin*); dry land (*yabashah*), for it turned to shame (*habishah*) its good deeds when it accepted the blood of Abel; ground, for it fled from God's presence when He wished to give Israel the Torah at Mount Sinai;[18] world (*tebel*), for it is spiced with (*metubbelet*) fruits; abode (*ḥeled*), for sons of man decompose (*ḥaludim*) in it; beginning, for it was first of all the works of creation;[19] valley (*gay*), for it is made up of hill (*givʿah*) after hill;[20] field, for it is made up of field after field. R. Zeʿera inferred this latter derivation from the verse, *And Isaac went out walking in the field* (Gen. 24:63).

Now, sons, listen to me; happy are they who keep my ways (Prov. 8:32)— God said to Israel: My children, all I request from you is to listen this time only—*Listen to Me;* if you listen to me [this time] I will fulfill for you that which Isaiah the prophet had said, *If, then, you agree and give heed, you will eat the good things of the earth* (Isa. 1:19); if not, *you will be devoured by the sword; for it was the Lord who spoke* (Isa. 1:20).

Now, sons, listen to me (Prov. 8:32). This is what Solomon has prophesied, saying, *Happy is the man who listens to me, coming early to my gates day by day, waiting at the posts of my doors* (Prov. 8:34)—God meant, Happy is the man who listens to Me [and follows My advice] to study at my gates day by day. Why *day by day,* [repeating the word] twice? [To indicate the reward in] both worlds, this world and the world to come. Whoever listens to Me and comes early to the gates of My Torah will inherit the life of this world and the life of the world to come. *Waiting at the posts of My doors*—these are the portals of prayer, for one is obligated to betake himself early to the synagogue and enter it between its two sets of doorposts; only then may he stand in prayer.[21]

Another interpretation: *Waiting at the posts of My doors*—R. Tanḥuma said: One is obligated to affix a *mezuzah* to the doors of his house, as it is said, *Inscribe them on the doorposts of your house* (Deut. 6:9). R. Levi said: Two *mezuzot*, one on each side. R. Ishmael said: One *mezuzah*. The sages concurred with R. Ishmael.[22] Why so? Because if one had two *mezuzot* he would not know which is primary and which is secondary. R. Simon supported R. Ishmael, saying: It is written, *Bind them as a sign on your hands* (Deut. 6:8)—does it follow that one should have two phylacteries, one for each arm? If so, one would not know which is primary and which is secondary. Nevertheless [indeed for this very reason], the rule accords with R. Ishmael—just as the plural form of *mezuzah* refers to [only] one *mezuzah*, so the plural form of phylactery refers to [only] one phylactery [for the left arm only]. R. Yudan asked: If so, why is it said, *the posts of My doors* [in the plural]? So that if one has two doors he is obligated to affix a *mezuzah* to each one. Therefore it is said, *the posts of My doors* [in the plural].

For he who finds me finds life, and obtains favor from the Lord (Prov. 8:35). God said: Whosoever is found [studying] words of Torah will find Me in any place [that he seeks Me]. Therefore it is said, *For he who finds me finds life, and obtains (wayateq) favor from the Lord*—God said: Whosoever brings forth (*mefiq*) words of Torah and teaches them to the multitudes, I too shall bring forth [favor] for him at a favorable time. Therefore it is said, *obtains favor from the Lord.*

But he who misses me destroys his own soul; all who hate me love death (Prov. 8:35)—God said to the wicked: If you sin against Me, do you think in your souls that I suffer any loss? It is yourselves who suffer loss! Therefore it is said, *He who misses Me destroys his own soul.*[23] Not only that, but you think in your soul that you are gaining life for yourselves—you are only gaining death for yourselves! Therefore it is said, *All who hate Me love death.*

CHAPTER NINE

·   ·   ·

Wisdom has built her house, she has hewn her seven pillars (Prov. 9:1): This refers to the Torah, which built the entire universe through her wisdom. *She has hewn her seven pillars*—she was hewn from the seven firmaments[1] and was given to humanity. Another interpretation: *Wisdom has built her house*—God said: If one has earned the merit of teaching Torah to others, [I will account it to him] as though he had erected the entire universe. *She has hewn her seven pillars*—these refer to the seven lands. If one has earned the merit of upholding the Torah, he will inherit the seven lands; if not, he will be expelled from the seven lands.[2]

She has prepared the feast, mixed the wine, And also set the table (Prov. 9:2): *She has prepared the feast*—R. Abbahu said: This refers to Queen Esther. When great trouble befell Israel in the days of Mordecai, what did she do? She prepared a banquet for Ahasuerus and the wicked Haman and got them very drunk with wine. The wicked Haman thought to himself that she was paying him honor and did not realize that she had spread a net [to trap him], for in getting them drunk with wine she had preserved her people unto eternity. *She has also set the table*—she has furnished for herself a table in this world and a table in the world to come. What [sort of table] is this? It is the good name which she acquired both in this world and in the world to come, for all holy days will be annulled in the [messianic] future, but Purim will never be annulled, as it is said, *These days of Purim shall never cease* (Est. 9:28). R. Eleazar said: Nor will the Day of Atonement ever be annulled, as it is said, *This shall be to you a law for all time: to make atonement* (Lev. 16:34).[3]

Another interpretation: *And also set the table* (Prov. 9:2)—this refers to the Torah which furnishes a [rich] table for those who study it in this world and in the world to come. Another interpretation: *And also set the table*—a story is told of R. Aqiba who was confined in prison and was cared for by Joshua of Gerasa.[4] Once, on the eve of a holy day, Joshua took leave of his master and went home, whereupon Elijah the priest came by and stood at the door to his house, calling, "Come out, Joshua! Come out, Joshua!"[5]

Joshua asked, "Who are you?"

Elijah replied, "I am Elijah the priest, who has come to tell you that your master, R. Aqiba, has died in prison."

They both rushed off and found the gate of the prison open and the warden and everyone else asleep, while R. Aqiba was lying on his bed. Elijah took charge of him and hoisted the corpse upon his shoulder, whereupon Joshua of Gerasa said to him, "Did you not tell me, 'I am Elijah the priest'? Surely a priest is forbidden to render himself unfit by [contact with] a corpse!"[6]

Elijah replied, "Enough of this, Joshua, my son! God forbid—there is no unfitness attached to the righteous nor is there any in their disciples."[7]

Having left the prison they traveled all night until they reached the four-arched gateway of Caesarea.[8] When they arrived at the four-arched gateway of Caesarea, they went down some descents and up three ascents. There they found a bier spread out, a bench, a table, and a lamp.[9] They placed R. Aqiba's corpse upon the bier, and immediately the lamp was lit up and the table was set [of their own accord]. At that moment they exclaimed, "Happy are you, O ye laborers in Torah! Happy are you who fear God![10] Happy are you, R. Aqiba, for whom a good resting-place has been found at the moment of your death!" Therefore it is said, *And also set the table.*

Another story is told about the elders who were reclining at a banquet at the home of Rabban Gamaliel,[11] while Tabi, his slave, was standing by and serving him. R. Eleazar ben Azariah said: Woe unto you, O Canaan! For you have condemned your descendants [to slavery] whether they be righteous or wicked.[12] By right, Tabi should have been reclining and I should have been serving him.

R. Ishmael said: We find a greater person [than Tabi who had served inferior people, namely] Abraham. For Abraham, one of the greatest men in the world, had served the Canaanite traders.[13]

R. Tarfon said: We find an even greater [example], for the High Priest serves Israel on the Day of Atonement.[14]

Rabban Gamaliel said to them: You are dealing with the honor of flesh-and-blood, while you ignore the honor of the King of [kings of] kings, praised be He. The King of kings of kings has created His world, He makes the winds blow, the sun shine, the rain fall, the dew drop, the sprouts grow, and sets the table [with food] for each and every one, as it is said, *You spread a table for me in full view of my enemies; you annoint my head with oil; my drink is abundant* (Ps. 23:5). Why [does He do] all this? For the sake of the Torah. Therefore did Solomon prophesy in his wisdom saying, *And also set the table* (Prov. 9:2).

R. Jeremiah said: Come and see how great is the honor of the Torah. Not only does she furnish a table for the sages but she also gives them wisdom in addition to her own wisdom. Hence it is said, *Instruct a wise man, and he will grow wiser, teach a righteous man, and he will gain in learning* (Prov. 9:9). If you see a disciple of the sages to whom the words of Torah are dear, give him [some of your own] wisdom, *and he will grow wiser, teach a righteous man, and he will gain in learning,* for being a righteous man prepared even to bring harm upon himself just so he can hear words of Torah, he thereby adds to his fear [of God], as it is said, *The beginning of wisdom is fear of the Lord, and knowledge of the Holy One is understanding* (Prov. 9:10).

The beginning of wisdom is fear of the Lord—this refers to the Torah; awe for it is incumbent upon the entire world. *And knowledge of the Holy One is understanding*—these are the masters of the Talmud, for when they sit down to explicate each and every matter contained therein, they resemble the ministering angels who are likewise called holy ones, [as it is said, *And judgment was rendered in favor of*] *the holy ones of the Most High* (Dan. 7:22). Where [is the scriptural proof that] sages are called holy ones? In the verse, *As to the holy and mighty ones that are in the land, my whole desire concerning them is that* (Ps. 16:3).

Four are called mighty:

God is called Mighty, as it is said,
The Lord on high is mighty (Ps. 93:4);

Israel are called mighty, as it is said,
As to the holy and mighty ones, my whole desire concerning them is that (Ps. 16:3);

Waters are called mighty, as it is said,
Above the thunder of the mighty waters (Ps. 93:4);

Egypt is called mighty, as it is said,
[Egypt,] along with the women of the mighty nations (Ezek. 32:18).

[Thus you find that]

Revealed was God	Who is called mighty
By the hand of Israel	who are called mighty;
God punished the Egyptians	who are called mighty
Through waters	that are called mighty,

as it is said,
They sank like lead in the waters mighty (Exod. 15:10).[15]

Another interpretation: *As to the holy and mighty ones, my whole desire concerning them is that* (Ps. 16:3)—this refers to the sages who know the concerns of Torah. Another interpretation: *As to the holy and mighty ones*—these are Israel who are God's desire. Another interpretation: *As to the holy and mighty ones*—these are Israel who desire the commandments of the Torah. Another interpretation: *As to the holy and mighty ones*—God said: So long as they do what I desire, I too shall do what they desire.

It is taught in the Mishnah: R. Eleazar said: Do His will in doing your will, so that He may do your will in doing His will. And give up your will before His will so that He may give up the will of others for the sake of your will.[16]

Hence David said, *But all is from You, and it is your gift that we have given to You* (1 Chron. 29:14). If you do so, He will lengthen your days and add to your years, as it is said, *For through Me your days will increase, and years be added to your life* (Prov. 9:11).

What follows this verse? *If you are wise, you are wise for yourself; if you are a scoffer, you bear it alone* (Prov. 9:12). Let me tell you a parable: To what may this matter be likened? To a poor man and a rich man; the rich man would say to the poor man every day, "How much property do you own? How many gardens and orchards do you have?" And the poor man would answer him saying, "Even though you own all this wealth, I get no benefit from it. All that you have acquired you have acquired for yourself!"

So God responds to the sage and tells him, My son, even though you have acquired wisdom, you have acquired it for yourself.[17]

If you are wise, you are wise for yourself. R. Eliezer used to expound [this verse], saying, *If you are wise, you are wise for yourself*—if you became wise in Torah it is as though you have caused God who gave you wisdom to rejoice, as it is said, *If you are wise, you are wise for your Self*—because of the Self Who gave you wisdom. *If you are a scoffer, you bear it alone*—if you have raised yourself as a scoffer, you must bear the blame alone and not [blame] others.

Another interpretation: *If you are wise, you are wise for yourself*—this is what is said to the disciples of the sages. It is taught in the Mishnah: If you have labored in the Torah there is a great reward to be given to you; but if you have neglected the Torah, I have many neglected things [to bring] against you.[18] Another interpretation: *If you are a scoffer, you bear it alone*—a fool may be compared to a promiscuous woman. Just as the fool is boastful and riotous in his folly, so is the promiscuous woman boastful and riotous in her promiscuity. Just as the fool does not realize what will be the end of his folly, so the promiscuous woman does not know what will be the end of her promiscuity, as it is said, *The stupid woman is riotous, she is thoughtless and knows nothing* (Prov. 9:13).

Another interpretation: *The stupid woman is riotous, she is thoughtless* (Prov. 9:13)—this refers to Eve, who listened to the serpent and transgressed God's command. Not only that, but she also caused Adam to sin. What follows this verse? *She sits in the doorway of her house, or on a chair at the heights of the town, calling to all wayfarers who go about their own affairs* (Prov. 9:14–15). This shows that she offered repentance to the [future] generations,[19] saying, "Whoever's ways are right will not sin as I have sinned! Woe unto anyone whose ways are not right, for he will become as culpable as I," as it is said, *Let the thoughtless enter here; And to the devoid of sense, she speaks to him* (Prov. 9:16). Let anyone lacking in knowledge learn from me, [said Eve,] for I stealthily deluded[20] God and I stealthily deluded Adam, and found this sweet for a while, but afterwards it was bitter, as it is said, *Stolen waters are sweet, and bread eaten furtively is tasty* (Prov. 9:17). Where [is the scriptural proof that] it was bitter in the end? In the verse, *He does not know that the shades are there, that her guests are in the depths of Sheol* (Prov. 9:18).

Even a sage who has intercourse with a married woman and, sinner that he is, finds momentary sweetness in it, does not realize that his end will be bitter, as it is said, *But in the end she is as bitter as wormwood, sharp, etc.* (Prov. 5:4). *And bread eaten furtively is tasty* (Prov. 9:17)—even when a man sins with a married woman in secret, saying, "None can see me," he does not realize that wherever he goes he has watchers with him to testify to his [wicked] deeds before God on Judgment Day in the coming future, as it is said, *He does not know that the shades are there, that her guests are in the depths of Sheol* (Prov. 9:18).[21]

In the end what does Scripture say? *Her guests are in the depths of Sheol.* Hence R. Ishmael used to expound this saying: Happy is the man who holds himself far from transgression and cleaves to the ways of God and to His wisdom. This shows you that when one cleaves to God's wisdom, he causes his Creator to rejoice. Therefore Solomon prophesied in his wisdom, saying,[22]

CHAPTER TEN

. . .

The Proverbs of Solomon.

A wise son brings joy to his father; a dull son is his mother's sorrow (Prov. 10:1). *A wise son* refers to Israel, as it is said, *You are children of the Lord* (Deut. 14:1); *brings joy to his father* refers to God, who is the Father of all the world, as it is said, *The father of orphans, the champion of widows* (Ps. 68:6). Another interpretation: *A wise son* refers to Solomon, who was very wise and caused God to rejoice in his wisdom; *a dull son is his mother's sorrow* refers to the wicked Haman, who listened to his wife and [as a result] was impaled on his stake, as it is said, *Then his wife Zeresh and all his friends said to him, "Let a stake be put up fifty cubits high . . . to have Mordecai impaled on it"* (Est. 5:14). And where [is scriptural proof] that he was impaled on his own stake? In the verse, *So they impaled Haman on the stake which he had put up for Mordecai* (Est. 7:10).

R. Nehemiah said: With all the wealth that he had, could he not have redeemed his life? [No, he could not.] This shows that when the moment comes for the downfall of an evil man, nothing can avail him, as it is said, *Ill-gotten wealth is of no avail, but righteousness saves from death* (Prov. 10:2).

R. Eliezer ben Jacob says: One verse reads, *Righteousness saves from death* (Prov. 10:2), while another verse reads, *What man can live [and not see death?]* (Ps. 89:49)—how may these two verses be reconciled? Only by assuming that *What man can live*, refers to death of a natural cause, while *righteousness saves from death* [means] that it saves those who practice it from unnatural death.[1]

Likewise, another verse [seems contradictory]. One passage reads, [God] *clears* [the guilty] (Exod. 34:7), while another passage reads, [God] *does not clear* [the guilty] (ibid.).[2] It is impossible to say [God] *does not clear* when it has already been said [God] *clears* [the guilty]. How then [may the two phrases be reconciled]? God clears the penitent but He does not clear those who are not penitent.[3]

It is taught there:[4] R. Mattiah ben Heresh said in the name of R. Ishmael: There are four kinds of atonement [which may be achieved]. They are these:

54

(1) if one transgresses a positive commandment in the Torah and repents, God immediately forgives him, as it is said, *Turn back, O rebellious children, I will heal your afflictions* (Jer. 3:22); (2) but if one transgresses a negative commandment and repents, his repentance [merely] suspends [the sentence] until [the next] Day of Atonement effects his repentance, as it is said, *It is a Day of Atonement* (Lev. 23:28); (3) if one commits a transgression involving the penalty of extirpation or death, repentance and the Day of Atonement effect atonement accompanied by suffering, as it is said, *I will punish their transgression with the rod, their iniquity with plagues* (Ps. 89:33); (4) but if the Name of Heaven has been profaned at his hand, neither does repentance have the power to suspend [his sentence], nor has the Day of Atonement the power to atone [for him], rather, repentance and the Day of Atonement suspend [his sentence until] death cleanses him, as it is said, *Then the Lord of Hosts revealed Himself to my ears: "This iniquity shall not be forgiven you until you die," said my Lord, God of Hosts* (Isa. 22:14).

Is it possible that even his death might not atone for him? [No, for] Scripture states, *I am going to open your graves, and lift you out of the graves, O My people, and bring you to the land of Israel* (Ezek. 37:12). R. Eliezer asked R. Joshua,[5] "What is this verse talking about?"

R. Joshua replied, "About those who die outside of the Land of Israel."

R. Eliezer then asked, "And what does it say about those who die in the Land of Israel?"

[R. Joshua replied,] "Their land will atone for them,[6] as it is said, *The land of His people makes expiation* (Deut. 32:43)."

R. Eliezer said, "What about the righteous? If they have sinned, will the Land atone for them, too?"

R. Joshua answered, "My son, if it atones for the wicked ones, is it not an inference from the minor to the major [that it will atone] also for the righteous? Come and see what Solomon has said in his Wisdom, that the righteous will not depart from this world until the Omnipresent has forgiven them all their sins,[7] as it is said, *The Lord will not let the righteous go hungry*—meaning that he will depart to his [future] world[8] free of sin; *but He denies the wicked what they crave* (Prov. 10:3)—for He thrusts them away for Judgment Day."

Another interpretation: *The Lord will not let the righteous go hungry*—he participates in life [eternal through his study of] words of Torah. If even one word or one paragraph of his studies remains hidden from him, he is taught it at the time for his departure from the world, for he does not depart until the ministering angels come and review it[9] with him, so that he will not be put to shame before God in the future to come.[10] Therefore it is said, *The Lord will not let the righteous go hungry.*

Another interpretation: *The Lord will not let the righteous go hungry*—R. Simon said: This refers to the righteous, whom God does not cause to be wanting even in their lifetimes.[11] *But He denies the wicked what they crave*—R. Abbahu said: This refers to the wicked, for God seals the decree of judgment against them before the hour of Judgment Day.[12] Why so? So that He may exact punishment from them with the torment of Gehenna. Therefore it is said, *He denies the wicked what they crave,* for he thrusts them away to the Prince of Gehenna.

Another interpretation: *The Lord will not let the righteous go hungry*—as long as he observes the way of life, for life means Torah, as Scripture says, *She is a tree of life to those who grasp her* (Prov. 3:18). And where [is the scriptural proof that] the disciple of the sages must observe [the way of Torah]? In the verse, *He who follows discipline shows the way to life, but he who ignores reproof leads astray* (Prov. 10:17). R. Alexandri said: Any disciple of the sages who abandons the words of Torah is considered as though he were trifling with Him who spoke and the world came into being.[13] Not only that, but once he abandons the words of Torah in this world, God will abandon him in the world to come. Therefore it is said, *He who ignores reproof leads astray.*

R. Ishmael said: Come and see how severe is [such] judgment, for God will judge the entire world in the valley of Jehosaphat.[14] When a disciple of the sages comes before Him, He will ask him, "My son, did you study Torah at all?"

The disciple will reply, "Yes."

God will then say to him, "Since you admit this to Me, tell me what you have read and recited[15] in the academy."

Hence the sages have said, Anything that a person has read[16] should be well grasped, and anything that a person has recited should be well grasped,[17] so that he may not be overtaken by shame and disgrace on Judgment Day. Hence R. Ishmael used to say: Woe for that shame! Woe for that disgrace![18] It was about this that David, king of Israel, prayed and supplicated God, saying, *Hear my voice, O Lord, at daybreak [at daybreak will I order my prayer before You and will look forward]* (Ps. 5:4).[19]

If the person who comes before God has [knowledge of] Scripture in hand, but none of Mishnah,[20] God turns His face away from him, whereupon the wardens of Gehenna overpower him like wolves of the steppe,[21] fall upon him, and fling him into its midst.

If the person who comes before God has [knowledge of] two or three orders [of the Mishnah] in hand,[22] God asks him, "My son, why did you not recite all of the laws of the Mishnah?" If God then says [to the wardens of Gehenna], "Let him be," well and good; if not, they do to him as they had done to the person before him.

If the person who comes before God has [knowledge of all] the rules [of the Mishnah] in hand, God asks him, "My son, why did you not recite the Midrash on the Book of Leviticus?²³ It deals with the unfitness and fitness of creeping things,²⁴ of plague spots,²⁵ of bald spots,²⁶ of houses,²⁷ of persons afflicted with flux,²⁸ of women after childbirth,²⁹ and of lepers,³⁰ as well as with the order of confession on the Day of Atonement,³¹ analogies from verbal congruities,³² and rules of valuation³³—in fact, every rule which Israel had instituted³⁴ has been derived from it.

If the person who comes before God has [the knowledge of] the Midrash on Leviticus in hand, God says to him, "My son, why have you not recited [the Midrashim on all] the Five [Books of the Pentateuch]?³⁵ They deal with the Shemaᶜ prayer, phylacteries, blue thread [in ritual fringes],³⁶ and *mezuzah.*"³⁷

If the person who comes before God has [the knowledge of the] Midrashim on all of the Pentateuch in hand, God asks him, "My son, why did you not recite haggadah? For whenever a sage is sitting and expounding [haggadah], I forgive and grant atonement for the sins of all Israel. Not only that, but when they respond, 'May His Great Name be praised,'³⁸ I forgive and grant atonement even for a judgment rendered [against them] many years ago [and not yet executed]."

If the person who comes has [the knowledge of] haggadah in hand, God asks him, "My son, why have you not recited the Talmud?" For the verse *All streams run into the sea, yet the sea is never full* (Eccles. 1:7) refers to the Talmud.

If the person who comes has [knowledge of] the Talmud in hand, God says to him, "My son, having studied Talmud, have you gone on to speculate on the glory of Chariot mysticism?³⁹ I derive no greater pleasure from the world that I created than when the disciples of the sages sit and behold and look and see and contemplate⁴⁰ the recitation of all this great teaching. What is [the nature of] My throne of glory? How does the first leg [of the throne] function? How does the second leg function? How does the third leg function? How does the fourth leg function?⁴¹ How does the electrum stand?⁴² How many revolutions per hour does it turn? In what direction does it function? How does the lightning stand?⁴³ How many aspects of radiance may be seen between His shoulders? In what direction does it function? How does Venus function?⁴⁴ In what direction does it function?

Greater than all, how does Rigyon beneath My throne of glory stand?⁴⁵ Is it round? Is it like a well-formed brick?⁴⁶ How many bridges are upon it? What is the distance between one bridge and another? When I cross over, which bridge shall I use? Which bridge do the [angelic] Wheels⁴⁷ use? Which bridge do the wheels of the Chariot⁴⁸ use?

More important than these, how do I stand, from My [toe]nails to the top of My head? What is the measure of My hand's span? What is the measure of My foot?[49]

Most important of all, how was My Throne of Glory [used during creation]?[50] In what direction did it function on the first day of the week [of creation]? In what direction did it function on the second day of the week [of creation]? In what direction did it function on the third day of the week [of creation]? In what direction did it function on the fourth day of the week [of creation]? In what direction did it function on the fifth day of the week [of creation]? In what direction did it function on the sixth day of the week [of creation]?

Is this not My glory? Is this [not] My greatness? Is this [not] My might? Is this not My splendor? Is this [not] the splendor of My beauty that My children recognize My glory by this measurement?[51] Of this David said, *How many are the things You have made,*[52] *O Lord* (Ps. 104:24)!

Hence R. Ishmael said: Happy is the disciple of the sages who preserves his learning in his heart, so that he will have the wherewithal to answer God on Judgment Day. Therefore it is said, *He who follows discipline shows the way to life* (Prov. 10:17). But if he forsakes his learning and abandons it, he will be overtaken by shame and disgrace on Judgment Day, wherefore it is said, *But he who ignores reproof leads astray.* What does this mean, *leads astray?* R. Benaiah said: God will distance him from Himself.

Another interpretation: *He who follows discipline shows the way to life*— one should not say, "Since I have already become wise in Torah, I will now go and deal in money and properties." He does not realize that these will not help him at all, as it is said,[53]

CHAPTER ELEVEN

. . .

Wealth is of no avail on the day of wrath (Prov. 11:4). What then will avail him? Words of Torah, for they have been likened to life; hence it is said, *He who follows discipline shows the way to life* (Prov. 10:17). *But righteousness*[1] *saves from death* (Prov. 11:4): Does righteous charity indeed deliver one from the torment of Gehenna? There are those who give charity to people who deserve it [and there are those who mistakenly give it] to those who do not deserve it. Could it be that even if one gives [charity] to a gentile it would deliver him? [Apparently it would not.] Hence you must say that righteous charity can only refer to words of Torah, as it is said, *It will be therefore to our merit [if we observe faithfully this whole Instruction]* (Deut. 6:25). If one wishes, he may learn [about the lifesaving value of words of Torah] from what R. Jose said: May my portion be among the collectors for charity and not among the dispensers thereof, for he who receives [a contribution] knows from whom he received it, whereas he who disburses it does not know [the character of] the recipient.

R. Ḥanina ben Dosa said: The only true righteous charity is Torah; hence it is said, *Righteousness saves from death* (Prov. 11:4), since Torah has the power to deliver one on Judgment Day. Could it be that even if a disciple [of the wise] is guilty of transgressions, Torah will nevertheless deliver him on Judgment Day? Scripture replies, *The righteous one is rescued from trouble, and the wicked one takes his place* (Prov. 11:8), showing that Torah does deliver a disciple of the sages who is guilty of transgression. But what about a perfectly righteous person? R. Aqiba said: You must perforce say that it is his [righteous] deeds that will deliver him, as it is said, *The righteousness of the upright saves them; but the treacherous are trapped by their malice* (Prov. 11:6). And why [will] all of this [happen]? Because of the merit of words of Torah which are likened to righteous charity and life, as it is said, *Righteousness is a prop of life; but to pursue evil leads to death* (Prov. 11:19).

Is there really a person who will [deliberately] pursue evil to his own [harm] and death? [Obviously there is not.] Hence you must say this refers to one who spends day after day without Torah. R. Abbahu said: This refers to one who spends his days in scornful pursuits. R. Zeera said: This refers to one who spends his days in evil pursuits, as it is said, *But he who pursues vanities is devoid of sense* (Prov. 12:11). Scripture uses the expression *devoid of sense* here, and also in reference to transgression in the verse, *He who commits adultery is devoid of sense* (Prov. 6:32). Not only that, but he causes harm to himself at the time of death, wherefore it is said, *But to pursue evil [leads to death]* (Prov. 11:19)—[he brings it] upon himself, upon his own soul.

What is written thereafter? *Men of crooked mind are an abomination to the Lord, but those whose way is blameless please Him* (Prov. 11:20). *Men of crooked mind are an abomination to the Lord:* R. Joḥanan said: One who sets his mind against repentance, God calls an abomination, as it is said, *Men of crooked mind are an abomination to the Lord, but those whose way is blameless (temim) please Him.* Happy is he who puts an end (*tam*) to his sins and offers penitence, for God calls him blameless, as it is said, *But those whose way is blameless please Him.*

Another interpretation: *But those whose way is blameless please Him*—R. Tanḥuma said: Come and see Solomon's greatness and wisdom, for all that his father David had prophesied, he likewise prophesied.[2] In David's [works] it is written, *Happy is the man who is anxious always; but he who hardens his mind falls into misfortune* (Prov. 28:14);[3] [while] Solomon says, *Men of crooked mind are an abomination to the Lord* (Prov. 11:20). David says, *Happy are those whose way is blameless* (Ps. 119:1); [while] Solomon says, *But those whose way is blameless please Him* (Prov. 11:20). R. Zebidah said: God has said, "All who walk in blamelessness are considered by Me as though they had done My will (*reṣoni*)," as it is said, *But those whose way is blameless please Him (reṣono).*

Assuredly, the evil man will not escape, but offspring of the righteous will be safe (Prov. 11:21). Come and see: a man has two hands;[4] if he steals with one and gives charity with the other [thinking that the latter will atone for the former], he *will not escape.* Thus in the coming future God will say to the wicked, "I created two worlds for you, one in which to do good deeds and the other in which to receive a good reward [for them]. Now that you have done no [good] deeds in the world in which you were [living], you dare request a reward [here]! Consider that of man, whom I have created with two hands, and [who] transgresses with one hand and dispenses charity with the other, it is written, *Assuredly, [the evil man] will not escape;* yet you think that you will be spared the torment of Gehenna! [Mark you]—*the evil man will not escape!*"

R. Joḥanan said: Let me tell you a parable. To what may this matter be likened? To one who went off to commit a transgression by paying a harlot her price. No sooner had he left her doorway than a beggar accosted him, saying, "Give me some alms." He gave him [some money] and the beggar went on his way. The man then said [to himself], "Had God not wished me to atone for my transgressions, He would not have sent along that beggar so that I could give him some alms and thus atone for what I did." God replied to him, "O wicked one, think not so, but rather go and learn from Solomon's Wisdom, for he explicitly states in his Wisdom that *the evil man will not escape!*

Another interpretation: *Assuredly, the evil man will not escape*—R. Eliezer asked R. Joshua, "What is the meaning of *Assuredly, the evil man will not escape?*"[5]

R. Joshua replied, "Although one hand is nourished the same as the other, if a person performs a commandment with one hand and transgresses with the other, the one hand cannot atone for the other. Why so? Because *Assuredly, the evil one will not escape.* If a person engages in a deal between himself and another and he swears an oath with his mouth but annuls it in his heart, would you say that he will go unpunished? [No,] for Scripture says, *[The evil man] will not escape.* It is said here, *[The evil man] will not escape,* and it is said in the Ten Commandments, *[For the Lord] will not let escape [he who swears falsely by His name]* (Exod. 20:7). Just as the commandment there concerns a [false] oath, so the commandment here must refer to a [false] oath."[6]

R. Eliezer retorted, "Not so, for the end of the verse states explicitly, *But the offspring of the righteous will be safe* (Prov. 11:21). If you see a righteous man of good lineage, [you may be sure that] he will not quickly sin. Why so? For he will reflect [upon the consequences] saying, 'I had better suppress my inclination for the moment so as not to forfeit my [reward in the] world to come in the same moment.' He is thus saved from the torment of Gehenna. Therefore it is said, *But the offspring of the righteous will be safe.* The wicked person, however, will not reason in the same way, but will instead go to the harlot and swear an oath [to pay her full price] so that he may satisfy his lustful inclination, and forthwith violate his oath.[7] The holy spirit will respond to him, saying, 'O wicked one, it is not enough for you that you have committed a transgression—you also had to invoke My name for [your] lies! By your life, you shall not go unpunished by the torment of Gehenna!'"

R. Simon said, "Why does God call such a one evil? To correspond to the inclination to evil, which is [by definition] called evil, as it is said, *[And the Lord saw how great was man's wickedness,] nothing but evil all the time* (Gen. 6:5).[8] Therefore Solomon too called him evil, as it is said, *Assuredly, the evil man will not escape* (Prov. 11:21). *But the offspring of the righteous will be safe* (ibid.)—since God puts it in the hearts of the righteous not to sin, so that they may be saved from the torment of Gehenna, as it is said, *But the offspring of the righteous will be safe.*"

Like a gold ring in the snout of a pig is a beautiful woman bereft of sense (Prov. 11:22): If one puts a golden ornament in a pig's snout, the animal will proceed to befoul it with mud; will he not thus ruin it? So also, if a disciple of the sages goes to a harlot and satisfies his need with her, is he not besmirching his Torah? You cannot but say, "Yes, [he is]!" Hence it is said, *Like a gold ring in the snout of a pig is a beautiful woman bereft of sense.*

R. Alexandri said: What is the meaning of *bereft of sense?* She turns away the sense [learned by the study] of Torah from the disciple of the sages [who consorts with her]. But any [disciple] who can pass her doorway without lusting for her charms, God calls him righteous and good, as it is said, *What the righteous desire can only be good; what the wicked hope for [stirs] wrath* (Prov. 11:23). What is the meaning of *wrath?* R. Joḥanan said: [There is wrath in heaven] for he has destroyed his hope for the sake of a moment [of carnal pleasure].

One person gives generously and ends with more; another stints on doing the right thing and incurs a loss (Prov. 11:24)—R. Abbahu said: If you see a person scattering his money in alms, know that he will have more [wealth in the end], as it is said, *One person gives generously and ends with more.* R. Samuel bar Naḥmani said: If you see a person holding back from giving alms, know that he will become needy [in the end], as it is said, *another stints on doing the right thing.*

Another interpretation: *One person gives generously*—if you see a generation to whom words of Torah are precious, scatter them [lavishly] among them. *Another stints on doing the right thing and incurs a loss*—if you see a generation that longs for words of Torah, and you fail to teach them, in the end your own [knowledge of] Torah will be diminished. Why so? Because as you teach you learn, as it is said, *A generous person enjoys prosperity; he who satisfies others shall himself be sated* (Prov. 11:25).

He who satisfies others shall himself be sated: Not only that, but also any one who refrains from teaching words of Torah in this world, in the future to come the ministering angels will pierce[9] him full of holes like a sieve. 'Ula said: In the future even embryos in their mothers' wombs will curse such a one, as it is said, *He who withholds grain earns the curses of the people, but blessings are on the head of the one who dispenses it* (Prov. 11:26). *Grain (bar)* must refer to words of Torah, as it is said, *Pay homage in good faith (bar) lest He be angered* (Ps. 2:12). *The people* must refer to embryos in their mothers' wombs, as it is said, *Two peoples are in your womb* (Gen. 25:23).[10]

But blessings are on the head of the one who dispenses it (Prov. 11:26). R. Tanḥuma said: He who teaches Torah in this world will have a diadem upon his head in the coming future hence it is said, *But blessings are on the head of the one who dispenses it.*

He who earnestly seeks what is good pursues what is pleasing (Prov. 11:27): If you see a person who speaks well of another, the ministering angels will bespeak his merit before God, as it is said, *I will be gracious to him whom I consider gracious* (Exod. 33:19).[11] *He who is bent on evil, upon him it shall come* (Prov. 11:27): If you see a person who speaks ill of another, the ministering angels will speak ill of him before God, as it is said, *His mischief will recoil upon his own head* (Ps. 7:17).

He who is bent on evil, upon him it shall come (Prov. 11:27): This refers to the wicked Haman, who sought to do harm to Mordecai, but it was turned back upon him. What is written thereafter? *He who trusts in his wealth shall fall, but the righteous shall flourish like foliage* (Prov. 11:28). *He who trusts in his wealth shall fall*—this refers to the wicked Haman; *but the righteous shall flourish like foliage*—this refers to Mordecai and Esther.

Another interpretation: *He who trusts in his wealth shall fall*—this refers to Koraḥ; *but the righteous shall flourish like foliage*—this refers to Moses and his Sanhedrin.[12]

R. Levi said: There were two exceedingly wealthy men in the world, one among the Jews and one among the Gentiles. The one among the Jews was Koraḥ, and the one among the Gentiles was the wicked Haman. Both of them listened to their wives and fell [from power as a result].

How did it happen that Koraḥ fell [as a result of] listening to his wife? When he came home from the house of study, she asked him, "What ruling did Moses expound to you in the academy?"

He replied, "He explicated the law of the blue fringes."[13]

She asked him, "What are these blue [fringes]?"

He told her, "This is how Moses explained it: 'I have been told from the mouth of the Almighty that I should come and tell you to make four fringes on the four corners of your garments, and it will suffice [to fulfill your legal obligation] if it is of blue thread, as it is said, *Let them attach a cord of blue to the fringe at each corner*'" (Num. 15:38).

At this she burst out laughing and said to him, "See now how he sits and makes fun of you? Do you know what? He is telling you, 'on the corners of your garments'—I will make you a cloak that is all blue."

When Moses saw the blue cloak, he said, "O Koraḥ, what is this that you have made?"

Koraḥ replied, "You told me a little [blue], and I made it all [blue]."

Moses responded to him by saying, "It is written, *Inscribe them on the doorposts [of your house]* (Deut. 6:9). Does a house that is full of Torah Scrolls require a *mezuzah?*"[14]

Koraḥ said, "Of course!"

Moses went on, "Let your ears hear what your mouth is saying!" Then Moses said, "O Koraḥ, you have transgressed God's commandments because you have grown haughty in your wealth." Thereupon Moses stood in anger before God and spoke up before Him saying, "Master of the universe, if my words are to stand, pray issue a decree in their behalf," as it is said, *But if the Lord brings about something unheard of [so that the ground open its mouth and swallows them . . . And the earth . . . swallowed them up, with their households, all Koraḥ's people and all their possessions]* (Num. 16:30–32).[15] [Regarding the *something unheard of*] Moses said before God, "Master of the universe, if it has not yet been created, let it be created [now]." What was this [newly created thing]? It was the entryway to Gehenna.[16]

R. Levi said [explicating the names given to Koraḥ in Num. 16:1]: *Koraḥ (qoraḥ),* because he caused a loss of population (literally, "bald spot," *qorḥah*) in Israel;[17] *son if Izhar (yiṣhar),* because he caused [the temper of] the whole world to boil [until it was as hot] as noontime (*ṣohorayim*); *son of Kohath (qehat),* because he set on edge (*qihah*) the teeth of him who fathered him; *son of Levi (Lewi),* a son who led a procession (*lewayah*) to Gehenna. What caused him [all this trouble]? His trust in his riches [instead of in God]; hence it is said, *He who trusts in his wealth shall fall* (Prov. 11:28).

Where [in Scripture is the proof] that the wicked Haman listened to his wife and fell [from power as a result]? In the verse, *Then his wife Zeresh and all his friends said to him* (Est. 5:14). What did they say to him? *Let a stake be put up fifty cubits high* (ibid.). It is not written, "they made a stake," but rather, *let a stake be put up fifty cubits high;* this shows, said R. Levi, that they all participated in the advice. What did Haman do then? He arose in the morning to speak ill of Mordecai before Ahasuerus. After he had spoken before Ahasuerus, the king said to him, "Come and dine with me."

The wicked Haman said to himself, "Once I am seated with the king at the banquet, I will advise him to have Mordecai impaled on the stake."

The holy spirit responded, "O wicked one, your [evil] thoughts will be turned upon your own head."

And so it happened to him, as it is said, *So they impaled Haman* (Est. 7:10). This is also what is meant by the proverb, Woe to him who, as his house is destroyed, is hanged from his own beam. What caused all this to happen to him? His trust in his wealth; hence it is said, *He who trusts in his wealth shall fall* (Prov. 11:28). To all his plotting the holy spirit kept responding, "Not according to your planning but according to My planning," as it is said, *For My plans are not your plans, nor are My ways your ways, declares the Lord* (Isa. 55:8).[18]

CHAPTER TWELVE

· · ·

R. Ḥama bar Ḥanina said: Anyone who chats with his fellow and eats and drinks with him, yet speaks ill of him, is branded by God as wicked, as it is said, *Deceit is in the minds of those who plot evil* (Prov. 12:20). On the other hand, anyone who neither eats nor drinks with another nor has any dealings with him, yet speaks well of him, is called by God a [counselor of] peace, as it is said, *For the counselors of peace there is joy* (ibid.).

R. Zeʿira discerned a different implication [in this verse]: Anyone who lies in his bed at night and schemes, saying, "Tomorrow I will get up early and do such-and-such to my colleague," is called wicked by God, as it is said, *Deceit is in the minds of those who plot evil* (ibid.). Another interpretation: *Deceit (mirmah) is in the minds:* R. Levi said: In the future, worms (*rimmah*) will reign over the heart of him who devises evil. But anyone who lies in bed at night and thinks, "Tomorrow I will wake up early and do a good turn for So-and-so," will rejoice with the righteous in the Garden of Eden in the coming future, as it is said, *For the counselors of peace there is joy.*

Rab Huna asked, "Why did Scripture see fit to say, *For the counselors* [in the plural] and not 'for the counselor' [in the singular]?" R. Levi replied, "These are man's two kidneys, which advise him, one to do good and the other to do evil.[1] The right one is for good and the left one is for evil, as it is said, *A wise man's mind tends toward the right hand, a fool's toward the left* (Eccl. 10:2), and so also does David say, *For the righteous God probes the hearts and kidneys* (Ps. 7:10). But does man also have two hearts? Hence you must conclude that *hearts* refers to the Inclination to good and the Inclination to evil. *Kidneys* refers to the two kidneys who are the ones that counsel him, hence it is said, *For the counselors of peace there is joy* (Prov. 12:20). Not only that, but they are also called righteous. When? At the time when they advise man to do good. Where [in Scripture] are they called righteous? In the verse, *Rejoice in the Lord and exalt, O you righteous; shout for joy, all upright men* (Ps. 32:11)."

No harm befalls the righteous; but the wicked have their fill of misfortune

66

(Prov. 12:21): *No harm*—at the time when he walks in his innocence; *but the wicked have their fill of misfortune*—this refers to the hypocrite.[2] Not only that, but God calls him an abomination, as it is said, *Lying speech is an abomination to the Lord, but those that act faithfully please Him* (Prov. 12:22), [the latter half of the verse] referring to him who does business in [good] faith.

A clever man conceals what he knows, but the mind of a dullard cries out folly (Prov. 12:23): *A clever man conceals what he knows* refers to one who is not haughty about his Torah learning; *but the mind of a dullard cries out folly* refers to one who is haughty in his opinions. R. Ze'ira discerned a different implication from the verse: *Every clever man acts knowledgeably* (Prov. 13:16) refers to one who is not haughty in his wisdom; *but a dullard exposes his stupidity* (ibid.) refers to one who is haughty in his folly.[3]

CHAPTER THIRTEEN

. . .

And so does Scripture say, *He who keeps company with the wise becomes wise; but he who consorts with dullards comes to grief* (Prov. 13:20). A parable: To what may this be likened? To one who enters a perfumer's shop—even if the owner sells him nothing, nor does he buy anything from the owner, after he leaves his person and his clothing are scented, nor does the scent leave him all day long. It is of such a one Scripture says, *He who keeps company with the wise becomes wise; but he who consorts with dullards comes to grief.* [Another parable: To what may this be likened?] To one who enters a tanner's shop—even if the owner sells him nothing, nor does he buy anything from the owner, after he leaves his person and his clothing are evil-smelling. Nor does the stench leave him all day long. It is of such a one that Scripture says, *But he who consorts with dullards comes to grief.*

So also for anyone who walks with a sage; all who see him would say, "Were he not himself a sage, he would not be walking with another person who is likewise a sage." And anyone who walks with a fool; all who see him would say, "Were he not a fool, he would not be walking with another person who is likewise a fool." Hence it is said, *He who keeps company with the wise becomes wise, etc.*[1]

What is written following this? *Misfortune pursues sinners; but the righteous are well rewarded* (Prov. 13:21): *Misfortune pursues sinners,* them and their children, and their children's children; *the righteous are well rewarded,* to them and to their children and to their children's children. What is written following this? *A good man has what to bequeath to his grandchildren for the wealth of sinners is stored up for the righteous* (Prov. 13:22); wherefrom you learn that he bequeaths his goodness to his children and to his children's children.

The tillage of the poor yields much food; but substance is swept away for lack of moderation (Prov. 13:23)—R. Simeon ben Yoḥai [commented]: In this world the rich consume the poor, but in the coming future God will demand it from him, as it is said, *"Because of the groans of the plundered poor and needy, I will now act," says the Lord* (Ps. 12:6). God will say, "The time has come for Me to demand from you *because of the groans of the plundered poor and needy,* [which is to say, that you restore] what you have stolen and [pay a penalty for] having troubled them." R. Jose the Galilean said: Not so; rather, if a person has committed robbery and theft in this world, [his punishment will not be delayed until he dies]. Instead, he will not depart from his world until others despoil him. Whence in Scripture do we learn this? From the end of the same verse, *But substance is swept away for lack of moderation:* just as he had done unjustly [unto others in the past], so shall others do unjustly unto him [before he dies].[2]

He who spares the rod hates his son, but he who loves him disciplines him early (Prov. 13:24): Is there really a man who hates his son? Rather, [what the verse means is] that he who does not spank his son for violation of [common] wisdom or proper behavior is considered the same as if he hated him. If, however, he does spank him for violation of words of Torah or of proper behavior, he is regarded as one who loves him. Hence it is said, *But he who loves him disciplines him early.*

R. Eliezer said: Because God loves the righteous, He chastises them in this world, as it is said, *But He who loves him disciplines him early.*[3] R. Eliezer said further: Because God loves Israel, He disciplines them by handing them over to enslavement by the [four] kingdoms[4] in this world, so that they will thereby achieve atonement for their sins in the coming future, as it is said, *But He who loves him disciplines him early.*

The righteous person eats to his heart's content, but the belly of the wicked is empty (Prov. 13:25): *The righteous person eats to his heart's content*—this refers to one who fills himself with words of Torah; *but the belly of the wicked is empty*—this refers to him who has absorbed no words of Torah. Another interpretation: *The righteous person eats to his heart's content*—even if he has studied Torah in his youth, he may not sit idly in his old age, but should spend all his days filling himself with words of Torah; *but the belly of the wicked is empty*—if a person had studied Torah in his youth but then forgot it, if he does not go over it again in his old age, God will deny him the goodness of the Garden of Eden in the coming future, for He will say to him in the coming future, "Because you have denied yourself words of Torah in the world in which you were, I am denying you the goodness which I have laid away for the righteous in the coming future."

R. Levi said: Come and see how great is the treasure that God has laid up for the righteous for the coming future, as it is said, *How abundant is the goodness which You have in store for those who fear You; that You do in the full view of men for those who take refuge in You* (Ps. 31:20). Scripture says not "in the sight of Him and them" but *in the full view of men*—before all of the inhabitants of the world.

R. Joḥanan said: Not so; rather, [ordinarily] one can show the eye only that which it can see, and make the ear listen only to that which it can hear. But what God has prepared for the righteous in the coming future, no eye can behold it nor can any ear hearken to it, as it is said, *No eye has seen, O God, but You, who act for those that trust in You* (Isa. 64:3).[5]

CHAPTER FOURTEEN

·   ·   ·

The wisest of women builds her house (Prov. 14:1)—This refers to Jochebed, who raised three righteous children in the world: Moses, Aaron, and Miriam. All three attained the merit of serving Israel, and all three served as providers for Israel: Moses provided the manna, Aaron provided the clouds of glory, and Miriam provided the well.[1] All three were prophets. Where [in Scripture is the proof for the prophecy of] Moses? In the verse, *Never again did there arise in Israel a prophet like Moses* (Deut. 34:10). Where [in Scripture is the proof for the prophecy of] Aaron? In the verse, *With your brother Aaron as your prophet* (Exod. 7:1). Where [in Scripture is the proof for the prophecy of] Miriam? In the verse, *Then Miriam the prophetess, Aaron's sister, took a timbrel in her hand* (Exod. 15:20).

R. Huna said: What did Miriam prophesy? She told her father, "You will bear a son who will arise and save Israel." After Moses was born and was cast into the Nile, her father said to her, "My daughter, where is your prophecy [now]?"[2] She nevertheless held firm to her prophecy, as it is said, *And his sister stood at a distance [to learn what would befall him]* (Exod. 2:4).[3] *Stood* refers to [the manifestation of] the holy spirit,[4] as it is said, *I saw my Lord standing by the altar* (Amos 9:1); *his sister* likewise refers to [the manifestation of] the holy spirit, as it is said, *Say to wisdom, "You are my sister"* (Prov. 7:4); *at a distance* again refers to [the manifestation of] the holy spirit, as it is said, *The Lord revealed Himself to me in the distance* (Jer. 31:3); *to learn* once more refers to [the manifestation of] the holy spirit, as it is said, *For the Lord is an all-knowing God* (1 Sam. 2:3); *what would befall him* refers to [the same manifestation of] the holy spirit, as it is said, *Indeed, my Lord God does nothing without having revealed His purpose to His servants the prophets* (Amos 3:7).

R. Eleazar said: As a reward for Moses having led the men in [his] Song [of the Sea], Miriam led the women in [her] Song [of the Sea], [as it is written of] Moses, *Then Moses and the Israelites sang this song* (Exod. 15:1), and so too, of Miriam, *And Miriam sang for them* (Exod. 15:21).

But folly tears it down with its own hands (Prov. 14:1): This refers to the wicked Zeresh, wife of the wicked Haman.

Another interpretation: *The wisest of women builds her house*—R. Abbahu said: Anyone who has acquired wisdom in this world may be assured that he has acquired thereby a home in the world to come. *But folly tears it down with its own hands*—anyone who has not acquired wisdom in this world may be assured that he has acquired Gehenna in the coming future.

Another interpretation: *The wisest of women builds her house*—as a reward for conduct in fear of heaven, God gives a person wisdom, as it is said, *He who maintains his integrity fears the Lord; a man of devious ways scorns Him* (Prov. 14:2).[5] And having earned the merit of fearing [God], he earns the merit of having his days lengthened, as it is said, *Fear of the Lord is a fountain of life, enabling one to avoid deadly snares* (Prov. 14:27)—once he distances himself from matters [of sin] so as not to become ensnared in them on Judgment Day, as it is said, *enabling one to avoid deadly snares.*

A numerous people is the glory of the king; without a nation a ruler is ruined (Prov. 14:28)—R. Ḥama bar Ḥanina said: Come and see the praiseworthiness and greatness of God, for although there are before Him a thousand thousand and ten thousand myriads of ministering angels to serve Him and praise Him, He desires not the praise of all these but only the praise of Israel, as it is said, *A numerous people is the glory of the king*—*people* here must mean Israel, as it is said, *The people I formed for Myself* (Isa. 43:21). Why so? So that they might tell His praise in the world, as it is said, *That they might declare My praise* (ibid.).

Scripture also says, *The great of the peoples are gathered together, the retinue of Abraham's God; for the guardians of the earth belong to God; He is greatly exalted* (Ps. 47:10)—R. Simon said: When is God exalted in His world? When Israel gather in synagogues and houses of study and give praise and acclaim before their Creator. R. Ishmael said: When they gather in the house of study and hear a word of haggadah from the mouth of a sage, at the conclusion of which they respond, "May His great name be praised!"[6] At that moment God rejoices and is exalted in His world, and He tells the ministering angels, "Come and see this nation which I created for Myself, how they praise Me!" Whereupon the ministering angels invest Him with splendor and majesty. Hence it is said, *A numerous people is the glory of the king* (Prov. 14:28). *Without a nation a ruler (razon) is ruined* (ibid.)—[God said]: If they separate themselves from [the study of] words of Torah, I in turn will separate the Secrets (*raze*) of Torah from them.[7]

Wisdom rests quietly in the mind of a prudent man, but among dullards it makes itself known (Prov. 14:33)—R. Huna said: The former refers to the disciple of the wise who is the son of a disciple of the wise, whereas *among dullards it makes itself known* refers to the disciple of the wise who is the son of an unlettered father.

Righteousness exalts a nation; sin is a reproach to any people (Prov. 14:34): R. Joḥanan said: Come and see how great is the power of righteousness, for it is held in the right hand of God, as it is said, *Your right hand is filled with righteousness* (Ps. 48:11). Great is righteousness, for because of it our father, Abraham, was praised, as it is said, *And he believed in the Lord; and He counted it to him for righteousness* (Gen. 15:6), and *For I have singled him out that he may instruct his children and [his posterity keep the way of the Lord, by doing what is just and right, in order that the Lord may bring about for Abraham that which He has promised him]* (Gen. 18:19).

Great is righteousness, for because of it King David was praised, as it is said, *And David executed justice and righteousness among all his people* (2 Sam. 8:15). Great is righteousness, for because of it Solomon was praised, as it is said, *Praised be the Lord your God, who [delighted in you and set you on the throne of Israel. It is because of the Lord's everlasting love for Israel that He made you king, to administer justice and righteousness]* (1 Kings 10:9).

Great is righteousness, for it reaches the firmament of heaven, as it is said, *Your righteousness is like the high mountains; your justice [like the great deep]* (Ps. 36:7). Great is righteousness, for it reaches unto the throne of glory, as it is said, *Righteousness and justice are the base of Your throne*, etc. (Ps. 89:15). Great is righteousness, for because of it Israel was praised, as it is said, *And it will be righteousness to us*, etc. (Deut. 6:25). Great is righteousness, for because of it God will be praised on Judgment Day, as it is said, *And the Lord of Hosts is exalted by judgment [the Holy God proved holy through righteousness]* (Isa. 5:16).

Great is righteousness, for because of it God has been praised [for His promise] to bring salvation to Israel in the coming future, as it is said, *It is I who contend in righteousness, powerful to save* (Isa. 63:1). Great is righteousness, for it bequeaths honor and life to those who practice it, as it is said, *He who strives for righteousness and kind deeds, attains [life, success, and honor]* (Prov. 21:21). R. Levi said: Anyone who pursues righteousness and mercy in this world will find life, success, and honor on the day of his death.[8]

Great is righteousness, for because of it God will redeem Israel from among their [several] dispersions, as it is said, *Zion shall be redeemed with justice, and they that return of her with righteousness* (Isa. 1:27). Great is righteousness, for it accompanies him who practices it at the hour of his departure from this world, as it is said, *And thy righteousness shall march before you, the presence of the Lord shall gather thee in* (Isa. 58:8).

R. Simon said: This verse must refer to the death of Moses, as it is said, *And there came the heads of the people; he executed the righteousness of the Lord,* etc. (Deut. 33:21). R. Abbahu said: Come and see how agonizing it was at the moment of our teacher Moses' departure from this world. For at the time when God said to him, "Your time has come to take leave of this world," he began to wail and weep before God, saying, "Master of the universe, was it for naught that I have worn out [my] strength? Was it for naught that I have run like a horse before Your children? And now is the grave to be my end and my conclusion dust? If You deem me worthy, chastise me with sufferings but do not hand me over to the bonds of death." It is of this that David said, *Lord, punish me severely, but hand me not over to death* (Ps. 118:18).

God replied, "O Moses, I have bound Myself with an oath that no [earthly] reign shall overlap another even by a hair's breadth. Up till now you were king over Israel; now it is the time for Joshua to be king over them."[9]

Moses responded by saying before God, "Master of the universe, in the past I have been master to Joshua and he was disciple to me. Now let me be his disciple and he will be my master, just so I do not die."

God replied, "If you can do it, go ahead."

Moses went straight to Joshua's doorway and stood at Joshua's beck and call, his posture hunched and both his hands folded;[10] but Joshua did not even notice that our teacher Moses was standing there to serve him. The Israelites gathered at Moses' doorway, as they were wont to do, but did not find him. They asked, "Where is Moses?" and were told, "He went early to Joshua's doorway."[11] So they went forth and found Joshua seated while our teacher Moses stood at his side to serve him.[12]

They said, "O Joshua, Joshua, what is this that you have done? Your master Moses is standing to serve you! His posture is hunched, and his hands are folded!" At this Joshua's eyes were opened, and he beheld our teacher Moses standing to serve him. Forthwith Joshua prostrated himself before him, and weeping exclaimed, "My father, my father, my master, my master! My father who has raised me from my youth, my master who has taught me wisdom!"

Thereupon the sons of Aaron stood at Moses' right and Joshua stood at his left.[13] They asked him, "Our master Moses, what is this that you have done?"

He replied, "Leave me alone. God has told me, 'Do thus unto Joshua, and you will not die.'"[14]

R. Samuel ben Naḥmani said, quoting R. Joḥanan: At that moment all Israel sought to stone Joshua but the pillar of cloud [quickly] descended and interposed itself between Israel and Joshua.

Then the people said to Moses, "Complete the Torah for us." But the [concluding] traditions [of the Torah] were forgotten by Moses and he did not know how to answer. Having thus failed, he fell upon his face and said, "Master of the universe, *I would rather die than live* (Jon. 4:3)." When God saw that Moses had resigned himself to death, He composed a eulogy for him, as it is said, *Who will take My part against evil men? Who will stand up for Me against wrongdoers?* (Ps. 94:16)—who will stand up to Me in the battles against My children when they sin before Me?[15]

At that moment [the archangel] Michael came forth and prostrated himself before the Almighty, saying, "Master of the universe, Moses was Your own during his life, [to do with as You saw fit; surely] he is Your own in death!"

God replied, "I am not speaking of Moses but of Israel. So many times they sinned against Me, and he stood in prayer until he assuaged My wrath against them, as it is said, *He would have destroyed them, had not Moses His chosen one confronted Him in the breach, to avert His destructive wrath* (Ps. 106:23)."

Thereupon they came and announced to Moses, "The moment has come for you to depart from the world."

He said to them, "O Israel, my children, forgive me for all the pains which I have inflicted upon you."

They replied, "O Moses, our teacher, you are forgiven, you are forgiven." Then they said to him, "O Moses, forgive us for all the irritation that we have caused you."

He replied, "My children, you are forgiven, you are forgiven."

They came again and told him, "In one half-moment you must take leave of the world."

Moses raised his two hands and placed them over his heart, saying as he wept, "Of a certainty, these two hands that had received the Torah from the mouth of the Almighty, shall they fall off in the grave?"

They came once more and said to him, "The end of the moment for you to depart from the world has come."

It was then that he uttered a great cry before God and said to Him, "Master of both worlds,[16] if You take my soul in this world, will You return it to me in the coming future?"

God replied, "By your life! Just as you have been the head of all of them in this world, so will you be the head of all of them in the coming future, as it is said, *He came at the heads of the people* (Deut. 33:21)."

Why was all this [honor paid to Moses]? Because of the righteousness with which he treated Israel, as it is said, *He executed the righteousness of the Lord, and His decisions for Israel* (ibid.). R. Nehemiah said: What did he do? He taught them Torah, laws, and righteousness. Where is [the scriptural proof for]

Torah? In the verse, *Remember the Torah of Moses My servant, whom I charged at Horeb with laws and rules for all Israel* (Ma. 3:22). Where is [scriptural proof for] laws? In the verse, *See I [Moses] have imparted to you laws and rules* (Deut. 4:5). Where is [scriptural proof that Moses taught them] righteousness? *Righteousness, righteousness shall you pursue* (Deut. 16:20).

Hence Solomon praised Israel for [their] righteousness in his Wisdom saying, *Righteousness which exalts [the Israelite] nation, is a sinful reproach to the peoples* (Prov. 14:34).[17] That is, the [kind of] righteousness and deeds of love that the nations of the world perform are [accounted] to them as sin.

CHAPTER FIFTEEN

．　．　．

Better a meal of vegetables where there is love, than a fattened ox where there is hate (Prov. 15:17)[1]—R. Levi said: About whom did Solomon speak this verse? About two men [whom he met] when he fell from his royal estate and begged for a crust of bread from door to door in Israel. One time he met two men who recognized him. One of them approached and prostrated himself before him, saying, "My lord the king, if it please you, pray pay me notice [by dining with me] today." He thereupon brought him into his house, served him many delicacies, and began to recall to him stories of Solomon and his reign, saying, "Do you remember when you did such-and-such a thing on such-and-such a day, when you were king?" And as the host reminded him of the days of his reign, Solomon would weep and weep. This went on for the entire meal, until Solomon arose from the table sated with tears.

The next day the host's friend ran into Solomon and prostrated himself before him, saying, "My lord the king, if it please you, pray pay me notice [by dining with me] today." Solomon replied, "What do you wish to do to me? The same as your friend did to me yesterday?" He replied, "My lord the king, I am a poor man, but if you will pay me notice [by sharing] the bit of greens that I have, pray come with me to my house." Forthwith King Solomon went with him to his home. Upon arriving at his house, the poor man washed Solomon's hands and feet, served him the bit of greens, and began to comfort him, saying, "My lord the king, God swore an oath to your father David that kingship will not cease from his offspring, as it is said, *The Lord swore to David a firm oath that He will not renounce, "One of your own issue I will set upon your throne"* (Ps. 132:11). It is just God's way to chasten and then to turn about and assuage, as it is said, *For whom the Lord loves, He rebukes, as a father the son whom he favors* (Prov. 3:12). But God will surely restore you to your royal estate in the future."

When Solomon heard this he felt much better[2] and ate his fill of those greens. R. Hiyya bar Abba and R. Aboi ben Benjamin [said] quoting R. Jose ben Zimra: When Solomon was restored to his royal estate he prophesied con-

cerning it, saying, *Better a meal of vegetables where there is love* (Prov.
15:17)—better the dinner of herbs that I had at the poor man's home than the
fattened ox (ibid.) that I did not get to eat at the rich man's house and that
only reminded me of my troubles.[3]

A hot-tempered man provokes a quarrel; a patient man calms strife (Prov.
15:18)—R. Nehemiah said: *A hot-tempered man provokes a quarrel*—this refers to one who is short tempered; *a patient man calms strife*—this refers to
one who is long on patience. It is taught in a Mishnah: Who is mighty? He
who conquers his own inclination,[4] as it is said, *Better to be forebearing than
mighty, to have self-control than to conquer a city* (Prov. 16:32).

A wise son makes his father happy; a fool of a man humiliates his mother
(Prov. 15:20): *A wise son makes his father happy*—when he studies Torah; *a
fool of a man humiliates his mother*—this refers to the person who lapses into
an evil way of life.

The Lord is far from the wicked, but He hears the prayer of the righteous
(Prov. 15:29)—R. Hama bar Hanina said: Come and see how much more
severe is Solomon's wisdom than David's wisdom. Solomon's father said, *The
Lord is near to all who call Him [in sincerity]* (Ps. 145:18), while Solomon
said, *The Lord is far from the wicked* (Prov. 15:29). But [even David] stipulates,
to all who call Him in sincerity.[5] Hence *The Lord is far from the wicked* (Prov.
15:29) refers to those who offer no penitence at all, while *but He hears the
prayer of the righteous* refers to those righteous who pray for the [entire] congregation [and not only for themselves].

What brightens the eye gladdens the heart (Prov. 15:30): This refers to
words of Torah which cause a person's heart to rejoice, as it is said, *The pre-
cepts of the Lord are just, [rejoicing the heart; the instruction of the Lord is
lucid, making the eyes light up]* (Ps. 19:9). *Good news puts fat on the bones*
(Prov. 15:30)—just as words of Torah cause a person's heart to rejoice, so also
good news causes a person's heart to rejoice.

Another interpretation: *Good news puts fat on the bones*: A tale is told
about the Caesar, Vespasian, who came to destroy Jerusalem in the days of R.
Johanan ben Zakkai and announced to the inhabitants of Jerusalem, "Break a
bow or an arrow [and send it to me as a token of submission], and I will leave
you [alone]." This he told them, but they did not accept [his terms]. Right then
R. Johanan ben Zakkai said to them, "You are causing this city to be destroyed
and this House [of God] to be burned."[6] They replied, "Just as we have gone
out [and revolted] against former princes and slain them, so will we go out
against this one and slay him."

There were, however, pious and worthy men who documented everything
that R. Johanan ben Zakkai had said to them, wrapped the documents around

arrows, and shot them out of the city. They [the Romans] accordingly said, "R. Joḥanan ben Zakkai is a supporter of the Caesar."

As soon as R. Joḥanan ben Zakkai saw that the Jerusalemites would not accept his advice, he said to his disciples, "Arise and take me out of here." They put him in a casket, R. Eliezer taking hold of it at the head and R. Joshua at the feet. They solemnly went their way until they reached the gate of the city.

When they got to the gate of the city, they said [to the guards], "Arise and open [the gates] for us, so that we may go out and bury [this man]." The guards replied, "First we must pierce the casket [with our daggers] to ascertain whether he is alive or dead." The disciples retorted, "[If you do so,] you will cause a bad name to spread about your city, and people will say, 'They stab even a leading scholar.'"

In the end the guards stood aside and opened the gate. Once R. Joḥanan ben Zakkai realized that he had gone beyond the city gate, he went to greet Vespasian in the manner in which one greets royalty, saying, *Vive, Domine Imperator!*[7]

Vespasian asked him, "Are you the son of Zakkai?"

R. Joḥanan replied, "Yes."

Vespasian said to him, "You have [as good as] put me to death!"[8]

R. Joḥanan replied, "Fear not, for thus it is written [in the Scripture which is] in our hands, 'The Temple will be destroyed not by the hand of a commoner but by the hand of a king,' as it is said, *And the Lebanon trees shall fall by a mighty one* (Isa. 10:34)."[9]

Vespasian then handed him over to two prison guards. Three days later rescripts arrived for him from Rome, saying, "The Emperor Nero is dead, and the Roman people have chosen you to be emperor."[10]

Now when these rescripts arrived for Vespasian from Rome, he happened to be sitting in the bathhouse. He started getting dressed and put one boot on, but when he tried to put on the other boot, his foot would not go into it. R. Joḥanan ben Zakkai happened to be standing there, and Vespasian asked him, "What is the meaning of this [strange] event?"

R. Joḥanan replied, "The good news which you have heard has caused your flesh to swell. If you have an enemy, have him pass before you—your flesh will immediately subside and your boot will go on."

Vespasian did so, and his [other] foot went into the boot. He then asked R. Joḥanan, "Ben Zakkai, where does all this wisdom come from?"

R. Joḥanan replied, "From the wisdom of Solomon, for he says explicitly in his Wisdom, *Good news puts fat on the bones* (Prov. 15:30)."

Vespasian then said to him, "Ask for anything you may desire."

R. Joḥanan replied, "I ask for Yavneh[11] from you, so that I may study Torah there, make fringes, and fulfill there all of the commandments in the Torah."

Vespasian replied, "Behold, it is given to you as a gift."

He whose ear heeds the discipline of life lodges among the wise (Prov. 15:31): This refers to the disciple of the wise, for because he pays heed to the reproof of a sage, he acquires the merit to sit in the assembly of sages. If, however, he does not pay heed to the reproof of a sage, *he who spurns discipline hates himself; he who heeds reproof gains understanding* (Prov. 15:32): if he ruins himself [to acquire] words of Torah, he acquires heart—which is wisdom that is placed in the heart. Thereby he merits honor and humility, as it is said, *The fear of the Lord is the discipline of wisdom; humility precedes honor* (Prov. 15:33).

It is taught in a Mishnah: Heedfulness leads to cleanliness, cleanliness leads to purity, purity leads to holiness, holiness leads to fear of sin, fear of sin leads to [the gift of] the holy spirit, the holy spirit leads to resurrection of the dead, resurrection of the dead leads to the world to come, and the world to come leads to the Shekinah. Why [does] all this [occur]? Out of reverence, wisdom, honor, and humility; therefore is it said, *The fear of the Lord is the discipline of wisdom; humility precedes honor* (Prov. 15:33).[12]

CHAPTER SIXTEEN

. . .

A man may arrange his thoughts, but what he says depends upon the Lord
(Prov. 16:1): This is to let you know that everything is from God's hand, and
not from man, and both thoughts of the heart and what one says are from no
one but God. Another interpretation: *But what he says depends upon the
Lord*—any time a person pours out his supplication before God, He gives him
an answer to what he says, as it is said, *But what he says depends upon the
Lord.*

All the ways of a man seem right in his own eyes (Prov. 16:2): This refers
to the fool who considers himself wise in his own eyes and does not know that
The Lord probes motives (ibid.). But every one who casts out his own thoughts
and heart, God establishes his thoughts, as it is said, *Entrust your affairs to
the Lord, and your plans will succeed* (Prov. 16:3).

The Lord made everything for a purpose, even the wicked for an evil day
(Prov. 16:4): *The Lord made everything for a purpose,* referring to those who
labor in Torah; *even the wicked for an evil day,* for if he does not repent he is
made ready for the torment of Gehenna. *Every haughty person is an abomination to the Lord* (Prov. 16:5): This refers to him who [haughtily] elevates his
heart before his Creator. *Assuredly, he will not go unpunished* (ibid.)—he will
not escape the torment of Gehenna.

Rabbi Simon said: Every person who is of humble spirit and directs his
heart to walk in God's ways may be assured that He is directing his steps
[aright], as it is said, *A man's heart may plot out his course, but it is the Lord
who directs his steps* (Prov. 16:9).

There is magic on the lips of the king; he cannot err in judgment (Prov.
16:10)—R. Alexandri said: Solomon's wisdom is pleasing, for he taught wisdom to others from his own example. How so? Solomon said, "I call heaven
and earth to witness that [because of] all the wisdom that God has given me,
I did not let any falsehood depart from my mouth, rather all [that I said was]
in judgment," hence it is said, *He cannot err in judgment.*

Honest balances and scales are the Lord's; all the weights in the bag are

His work (Prov. 16:11): *Balance* refers to Scriptures; *scales* refers to [Rabbinic] judgments; *are the Lord's* refers to the Mishnah;[1] *all the weights in the bag are His work* refers to the Talmud; concerning all these, those who fulfill them will receive their reward in the world to come. R. Jose the Galilean said: [Let me tell you a] parable: To what may this be likened? To a king of flesh and blood who had a garden in which he built a tall tower. He showed affection for the garden by assigning workmen to it, and ordered them to busy themselves with its cultivation. The king thereupon ascended to the top of the tower, from which he could see them but they could not see him, as it is said, *But the Lord in His holy temple; be silent before Him all the earth* (Hab. 2:20).

At the day's end the king came down and sat in judgment upon them, saying, "Let the tillers come forward and receive their wages, let the hoers come forward and receive their wages," [and so on, until] there remained only those workmen who had done no work at all. The king asked, "These, what did they do?" They answered, "They emptied full vessels into empty ones." "What benefit is there for me in their emptying full vessels into empty ones?" asked the king, adding, "Let those who have done my work receive their wages, but those who did not do my work, let them be taken out and executed, for they have rebelled against my command!"

Thus also did God create His world and place mankind in it, commanding them to busy themselves with Torah, the commandments, and good works, while He caused his Shekinah to dwell in heaven, from which He could see them but they could not see Him. In the coming future God will sit in judgment saying, "All who have busied themselves with this [Torah], let them come forward and receive their wages," as it is said, *Where is the one who could count? Where is the one who could weigh? Where is the one who could count [all these] towers?* (Isa. 33:18). *Where is the one who could count?*—where are the teachers of little children who counted out [the letters of the alphabet for them]?[2] Let them come and receive their wages. *Where is the one who could weigh?*—where are those that weighed out [the logical premises, deducing from] the light to the weighty? Let them come and receive their wages. *Where is the one who could count [all these] towers?*—where are those who counted out the Midrashim on law and lore?[3] Let them come and receive their wages.

R. Ze'ira asked: And the wicked, what is God going to do with them? He will say to them, "O wicked ones, for naught, in vain have you spent your strength, seeing that you did not study the Torah. Why did you not busy yourselves with the commandments and good deeds? Instead you spent your time in My world like an empty vessel, which is of no use to Me. Neither are you yourselves of any use to Me." God will say further, "Are they perhaps to be dismissed and let go on their way scot-free? [Nay,] let them first see the rejoicing

of the righteous, and thereafter let them be consigned to the torment of Gehenna." Let me tell you a parable: To what is this to be likened? To a king who
gave a banquet and invited everyone but he did not set a time for it. Those who
were punctilious about the king's commands went off to bathe, and oil themselves, and iron their clothes, and thus got themselves ready for the banquet.
Those who were not punctilious about the king's commands plunged back into
their work. When the time came for the banquet, the king said, "Let everyone
come at once!" Those [who were punctilious] came in their glory while those
[who were not] came in their disgrace.[4] Thereupon the king said, "Those who
had prepared themselves for my banquet may partake of it; those who did not,
may not partake of it." Do you perhaps think that the latter would have been
dismissed and let go on their way? Rather the king went on to say, "Not so!
These shall eat, drink, and be merry while those shall stand upright watching
while they are being lashed and punished," as it is said, *Assuredly, thus said
the Lord God: My servants shall eat, and you shall hunger; My servants shall
drink, and you shall thirst; My servants shall rejoice, and you shall be shamed;
My servants shall shout in gladness, and you shall cry out in anguish, howling
in heartbreak* (Isa. 65:13–14).

What caused them [to come to this end]? Their failure to be punctilious
about the king's command, as Solomon explicitly said in his Wisdom, *A road
may seem right to a man, but in the end it is a road of death* (Prov. 16:25): *A
road may seem right to a man*—this refers to those who are punctilious about
God's commands; *but in the end it is a road of death*—this refers to those who
are not punctilious about God's commands.

Gray hair is a crown of glory; it is attained by the way of righteousness
(Prov. 16:31): If you see a person who clings firmly to the commandments, to
righteousness, and to almsgiving, he will earn the merit of gray hair, as it is
said, *It is attained by the way of righteousness.* Come and learn from [the example of] Joseph: because he stood [fast] in Egypt and held firm to his father's
honor,[5] he earned the merit of a hoary crown, as it is said, *Joseph lived to see
Ephraim's children of the third generation,* etc. (Gen. 50:23). Come and learn
from [the example of] David: because he earned the merit of honoring his
Sanhedrin,[6] he earned the merit of a hoary crown, as it is said, *King David was
now old, advanced in years* (1 Kings 1:1). Come and learn from Abraham:
because he paid honor to the ministering angels,[7] he earned the merit of a hoary
crown, as it is said, *Abraham was now old, advanced in years* (Gen. 24:1).

Why did all of this [come to pass]? Because *it is attained by the way of
righteousness* (Prov. 16:31). Where in Scripture do we find that each one prac-
ticed righteousness? Of Abraham it is written, *He reckoned it to him for righteousness* (Gen. 15:6); of David it is written, *David executed justice and*

righteousness among all his people (2 Sam. 8:15); of Joseph it is written, *Joseph sustained his father and his brothers* (Gen. 47:12). Thus you learn that old age can be attained only through righteousness, as it is said, *It is attained by the way of righteousness* (Prov. 16:31).

CHAPTER SEVENTEEN

. . .

Better a dry crust with peace, than a house full of feasting with strife (Prov.
17:1)—R. Joḥanan said: *Better a dry crust with peace*—this refers to the land
of Israel, for even if one eats but bread and salt therein each day, he is assured
of gaining life in the world to come; *than a house full of feasting with strife*—
this refers to the other lands, which are full of violence and robbery.

R. Joḥanan said: Anyone who walks but four cubits in the land of Israel is
assured of inhabiting the world to come. R. Levi said: Anyone who lives in the
land of Israel for even a year[1] and dies there is assured of inhabiting the world
to come. What is the [scriptural] proof [of this assertion]? *And the land of His
people makes expiation* (Deut. 32:43).[2] R. Neḥemiah said: [This verse refers
to] the land of Israel because it expiates the sins of its own dead [buried there].

R. Zebida asked: What then will you do with all of the righteous persons
who died outside of the land of Israel? Hence you must say that the land of
Israel will atone for its own dead, and that in the coming future God will
command the ministering angels to bring the righteous who died abroad
through underground tunnels[3] into the land of Israel, and there expiation will
be made for them, as it is said, "And I will purify them upon their land."[4]

R. Abbahu said: Would you also say that even the wicked who are in the
land of Israel will be atoned for [just by virtue of living there]? [No indeed,]
as it is said, *[So that it seizes the corners of the earth,] and shakes the wicked
out of it* (Job 38:13). And where will they be shaken into? R. Levi said: From
the land [of Israel] into the lands outside of it. R. Joshua said: God will never
let them rise again. R. Ishmael said: He will cause them to rise, so that they
will know that there is a [final] judgment and a [Supreme] Judge. [If so,] where
will He shake them into? Into Gehenna, as it is said, *The leech[5] has two daughters: "Give!" and "Give!"* (Prov. 30:15)—in the future to come Gehenna will
cry to God, "Give me the wicked!" It is taught in a Mishnah:[6] The sentence
of the wicked in Gehenna is [for no more than] twelve months.

R. Eliezer asked R. Joshua,[7] "Master, what should one do to be saved from
the torment of Gehenna?"

R. Joshua replied, "He should go and perform good deeds."

R. Eliezer asked, "If so, if the nations of the world also observe the commandments and perform good deeds, would they possibly be spared the torment of Gehenna?"

R. Joshua replied, "My son, the Torah speaks not of the dead [like the Gentiles],[8] but of the living."

R. Eliezer said to him, "May I offer you proof [for this statement]?"

R. Joshua said, "Speak."

R. Eliezer said, "One time I heard you expounding in the house of study, and you said,"[9]

CHAPTER NINETEEN

. . .

Better a poor man who lives blamelessly (Prov. 19:1): Anyone who lives blamelessly before his Creator in this world will be saved from the torment of Gehenna in the coming future. For so we find that Noah, who lived blamelessly, was called righteous, as it is said, *Noah was a righteous man; he was blameless in his age,* etc. (Gen. 6:9). Likewise we find that because Abraham lived blamelessly, as it is said, *Walk in My ways and be blameless* (Gen. 17:1), he earned the merit of acquiring both heaven and earth, as it is said, *Blessed be Abram of God Most High, creator of heaven and earth* (Gen. 14:19). [He merited heaven in that] his offspring deserved to inherit the Torah, which was given from heaven. And [he merited] the earth in that they deserved to be fruitful and multiply like the dust of the earth.[1] Why all this? Because of the blamelessness that he exhibited.

And so you find in every case where one had perfected his heart in blamelessness that God paired him off with an equally good counterpart. Thus we find in the case of Abraham that because he lived blamelessly, Sarah was paired off with him; and so also we find in the case of Isaac that because he lived blamelessly, Rebekah was paired off with him; and likewise in the case of Jacob we find that because he lived blamelessly, Rachel and Leah were paired off with him. All of these persons belonged to the same family and received the same [nonmaterial] inheritance. It is of them that Solomon spoke explicitly in his Wisdom, saying, *Property and riches are bequeathed by fathers, but an efficient wife comes from the Lord* (Prov. 19:14).

Why has all this [come to pass]? Because of the righteous charity which they, in their blamelessness, dispensed to the poor. God considered it as though they had dealt righteously with Himself, as it is said, *He who is generous to the poor makes a loan to the Lord; He will repay him his due* (Prov. 19:17), both in this world and in the world to come. Another interpretation: *He who is generous to the poor makes a loan to the Lord*—God said: Lend Me some charity in this world, and I will repay you in the world to come.

Another interpretation: *He who is generous to the poor makes a loan to the Lord*—God said: Lend Me some Torah in this world, and I will repay you in the world to come. R. Ishmael said:[2] This is the way of the Torah: if you eat [but] bread with salt, sleep on the ground, live a life of suffering, yet study Torah, *You shall be happy and you shall prosper* (Ps. 128:2). *You shall be happy*—in this world; *and you shall prosper*—in the world to come. Do not lust for the tables of royalty, for your table shall be more bountiful than theirs and your crown greater than their crown. [Furthermore,] He who hired your labor may be relied upon to pay you the wages of your work in full, [as it is said,] *He will repay him his due* (Prov. 19:17).

R. Ishmael said: Great is the Torah, for she is greater than priesthood and greater than kingship. For kingship is acquired through thirty qualifications, and priesthood is acquired through twenty-four qualifications, while the Torah is acquired through forty-eight: sitting, listening with one's ears, ordered speech,[3] cheerful countenance, good heart, intelligence, wisdom, awareness of one's place, acquisition of a colleague, punctiliousness in study, careful consultation of legal traditions, declaring the unfit unfit and the fit fit, making yes mean yes and no mean no, citing authorities by name—for all who cite authorities by name bring redemption to the world, as it is said, *And Esther reported it to the king in Mordechai's name* (Est. 2:22)—sharing the yoke [of study] with one's colleague, affording him the benefit of the doubt, receiving colleagues graciously, loving the sages' debate, rejoicing in study, not displaying hubris about one's learning, nor issuing decisions in the presence of one's master, nor sitting in the place of him who is greater [in learning], loving one's fellow creatures, loving [constructive] rebukes, admitting the truth, freely sharing knowledge of legal tradition, and handing one's child over to the study of Torah. Such a one may have hope for the future, as it is said, *Discipline your son while there is hope and do not set your heart on his destruction* (Prov. 19:18).

R. Joḥanan said: Every person who is a disciple of the sages, whose child is a disciple of the sages, and whose grandchild is a disciple of the sages [may be certain that] Torah will not cease from his family, as it is said, *[And the words which I have placed in your mouth] shall not be absent from your mouth, nor from the mouth of your children, nor from the mouth of your children's children—said the Lord—from now on, for all time* (Isa. 59:21). What is [the meaning of] *said the Lord?* R. Joshua ben Levi said: [It is as though] God said, "I am a guarantor on this matter." What is [the meaning of] *from now on, for all time?* R. Judah quoting Rab: From now on Torah will enjoy his hospitality.[4]

Many designs are in a man's mind (Prov. 19:21)—R. Jose the Galilean said: About whom did Solomon say this verse? He must have said it about his brother

Absalom,[5] who thought to himself, "If I slay my father David, I will have the kingship for myself." He did not know that God's designs would take precedence over his, as it is said, *Many designs are in a man's mind, [but it is the Lord's plan that is accomplished]* (ibid.). This refers [equally well] to Adonijah the son of Ḥaggith,[6] who took counsel with himself, saying, "I am greater than Solomon, and I am [more] fit for kingship." He did not know that God's counsel would take precedence over his.

Another interpretation: *Many designs are in a man's mind*, etc. (Prov. 19:21)—this refers to the wicked Haman, who thought to himself, "Tomorrow I will rise early and inform the king of Mordecai's deeds,[7] and the king will hand him over to me." He did not know that God's designs would take precedence over his, as it is said, *Many designs are in a man's mind, but it is the Lord's plan that is accomplished.*

[Another interpretation: *Many designs*, etc.] This refers to the wicked Pharaoh, who took counsel with himself, saying, "Behold, I will slay all the male Israelite [infants] so that they may not multiply and rise against me," as it is said, *[Then Pharaoh charged all his people, saying,] "Every boy that is born [you shall throw into the Nile]"* (Exod. 1:22). He did not know that God's designs would take precedence over his, as it is said, *But the Israelites were fertile and prolific; and [they multiplied and increased very greatly]* (Exod. 1:7). R. Zeʿira said: What is [the meaning of] *very greatly (meʾod meʾod)?* Double the number there had been.

It is written, *Catch us the foxes* (Song 2:15): this refers to the Egyptians; *the little foxes:* this refers to the Egyptian children, who were harder for Israel to bear than the adults, for one of them would enter the home of an Israelite, notice an infant, and forthwith denounce him; *that spoil the vineyards:* this refers to the tender Israelites; *for our vineyards are in blossom:* this refers to the sucklings.[8]

R. Simeon ben Yoḥai said: Why was Israel likened to a vineyard? In the case of a vineyard, in the beginning one must hoe it, then weed it, and then erect supports when he sees the clusters [forming]. Then he must return to pluck the grapes and press them in order to extract the wine from them. So also Israel—each and every shepherd who oversees them must tend them [as he would tend a vineyard]. Where [in Scripture] is Israel called a vineyard? In the verse, *For the vineyard of the Lord of Hosts is the House of Israel, and the seedlings he lovingly tended are the men of Judah* (Isa. 5:7).[9]

Just as in the case of a plant, from the moment you plant it, its place is recognizable, so too did God plant kingship in the Tribe of Judah until the Messiah shall sprout forth, as it is said, *The scepter shall not depart from Judah*, etc. (Gen. 49:10). R. Huna said: The Messiah has been given seven names, and these are: Yinnon, Our Righteousness, Shoot, Comforter, David, Shiloh, Elijah.

Where [in Scripture] is Yinnon? In the verse, *His name was Yinnon before the sun* (Ps. 72:17).[10] Where [in Scripture] is Our Righteousness? In the verse, *And this is the name by which he shall be called: Our Righteousness* (Jer. 23:6). Where [in Scripture] is Shoot? In the verse, *Behold a man called the Shoot, shall shoot out from the place where he is, and he shall build the Temple of the Lord* (Zech. 6:12). Where [in Scripture] is Comforter? In the verse, *For the Lord has comforted His people, and has taken back His afflicted ones* (Isa. 49:13). Where [in Scripture] is David? In the verse, *He accords great victories to His king, [keeps faith with his annointed, with David]* (Ps. 18:51). Where [in Scripture] is Elijah? In the verse, *Lo, I will send the prophet Elijah to you* (Mal. 3:23).

CHAPTER TWENTY

. . .

Wine is a scoffer, strong drink a roisterer; he who is muddled by them will not grow wise (Prov. 20:1): *He who scoffs at wine*[1]—this refers to words of Torah, for as R. Zeʿira said: Torah is likened to wine, as it is said, *Come, eat my food, and drink the wine that I have mixed* (Prov. 9:5). All who scoff at words of Torah are called scoffers, as it is said, *He who scoffs at wine.* Another interpretation: *Wine is a scoffer*—R. Joḥanan said: All types of beverages are efficacious for [curing the effects of] a dream, except for wine. Why so? Because if a person has merit, it will gladden him, but if not, it will devastate him. [Where is the scriptural proof that] if he has merit it will gladden him? In the verse, *Wine that makes glad the heart of men* (Ps. 104:15). And that if not it will devastate him? In the verse, *Wine is a scoffer* (Prov. 20:1).[2]

The terror of a king is like the roar of a lion: he who provokes his anger risks his life (Prov. 20:2). *The terror of a king is like the roar of a lion* —R. Judah, son of R. Simon, said: When peals of thunder sound in the world they rattle the whole of it; if peals of thunder have this effect, how much more so the roaring [voice] of God! Another interpretation: *The terror of a king is like the roar of a lion*—R. Ḥama bar Ḥanina said: When the young lion roars, a man who hears it is seized with fear; if so a lion['s roar], how much more so the roaring [voice] of God!

R. Levi said: The lion is called by seven names: lion, leo, young lion, lioness, mighty beast, roarer, and majestic beast.[3] [It is called] lion (*aryeh*), the usual; leo (*ari*), for all fear (*mityarʾin*) it; young lion (*kefir*), for all who see it despair (*kofer*) of their lives; lioness (*lavi*), for it snatches the hearts (*levavot*) of men; mighty beast (*layish*), for the flesh of men is like dough (*lish*) for its teeth; roarer (*shaḥal*), for all are terrified (*shoḥelim*) before it; majestic beast (*shaḥaṣ*), for it rends [its prey] asunder (*mashḥiṣ*) with its fangs.

Another interpretation: *The terror of a king is like the roar of a lion* (Prov. 20:2)—R. Huna said: Come and see how even the prophets were circumspect in their words,[4] as it is said, *A lion has roared, who can but fear? My Lord God has spoken, who can but prophesy?* (Amos 3:8). Could one possibly think

91

that His voice is no more [terrifying] than a lion's roar? You must retort: Who
was it that gave the lion its roar? Was it not He? So why all this [circumspection
in the words of the prophets]? Because they speak of Him in terms of His
creatures in order that the [human] ear may be bent to hear what it is able to
hear, as may be seen in the verse, *And there coming from the east with a roar
like the roar of mighty waters, was the presence of the God of Israel, and the
earth was lit up by His Presence* (Ezek. 43:2). Could [one possibly think] that
His voice was no more [awesome] than the sound of many waters? You must
retort: Who was it that gave sound to water? Was it not He? So why all this
[circumspection in the words of the prophets]? Because they speak of Him in
terms of His creatures in order that the [human] ear may be bent to hear what
it is able to hear.

Another example is the verse, *Now Mount Sinai was all in smoke [. . . the
smoke rose like the smoke of a kiln]* (Exod. 19:18). Could [one possibly think]
that His smoke was no more [intense] than the smoke of a kiln? Has it not
already been stated, *The mountain was ablaze with flames to the very skies*
(Deut. 4:11)? So why all this [circumspection in the words of Scripture]? Because it speaks of Him in terms of His creatures so that the [human] ear may
be bent to hear what it is able to hear.

Another interpretation: *The terror of a king is like the roar of a lion* (Prov.
20:2)—R. Ishmael said: Come and see the power and might of God—[of]
everything He created in His world, He affixed [a likeness] upon His throne
of glory. He created man and affixed [his likeness] upon His throne of glory;
He created the eagle and affixed [its likeness] upon His throne of glory; He
created the ox and affixed [its likeness] upon His throne of glory; He created
the lion and affixed [its likeness] upon His throne of glory.[5] When God raises
His voice in a roar, His throne of glory trembles. Why so? Because the likeness
of a lion is affixed upon it. Hence it is said, *The terror of a king is like the roar
of a lion*.

Who can say, "I have cleansed my heart, I am purged of my sin"? (Prov.
20:9): Let the name of the Holy, praised be He, be blessed for all eternity, for
purity and holiness is His, *Who tests the thoughts and the mind* (Jer. 11:20),
and He will purify Israel. Solomon said, "My father David said before God,
'Master of both worlds, *fashion a pure heart, O God* (Ps. 51:12).' He worded
this request inappropriately,[6] and as soon as he realized this he went back and
said, '*Wash me thoroughly from my iniquity, and cleanse me from my sin.*'"

How did the holy spirit answer him? It said, "O David, since you have
humbled yourself about the request which you had made [by rephrasing it], I
will grant it—I will create you a clean heart." Hence the holy spirit answered
him as he wished.[7]

When Solomon saw that his father David had humbled himself, he, too, said, *"Who can say, I have cleansed my heart?"* (Prov. 20:9). And what reward did he get for this? As it is said, *Solomon successfully took over the throne of the Lord* (1 Chron. 29:23). Now can any human being sit on God's throne? [Obviously not.] Rather, just as God's throne rules over the entire world, so did Solomon rule over the entire world, as it is said, *For he controlled the whole region west of the Euphrates—all the kings west of the Euphrates, from Tiphsaḥ to Gaza, and he had peace on all his borders roundabout* (1 Kings 5:4).

But are not Tiphsaḥ and Gaza next to one another? [Quite so, but the import of the text is that] just as one might leave Tiphsaḥ and [instead of going directly to Gaza] go East, then from the East to the West, then from the West to the North, and from the North to the South, thus encircling [the globe] until he reaches Gaza—so also did Solomon's rule encircle [the globe] from top to bottom.[8] R. Jose the Galilean said: Why did Solomon merit all this? Because he did not raise up his heart [in pride] before God. This is a matter of deduction from minor to major: if Solomon, king of Israel, father of wisdom, and father of prophecy humbled himself and thereby earned the merit of ruling from one end of the world to the other, how much more so does this apply to all other [lesser] persons. Hence the sages said: Happy is he who humbles himself and does not raise himself [in pride] in order to gain merit from God.[9]

CHAPTER TWENTY-ONE

. . .

Like channeled water is the mind of the king in the Lord's hand; He directs it to whatever He wishes (Prov. 21:1). R. Ishmael expounded this verse as follows: *Channeled water*—just as when you put water into a vessel you can tilt it to whatever side you wish, so also when flesh-and-blood is elevated to kingship, his heart is placed in God's hand [and may be influenced by Him as He wishes]. If the world merits it, God tilts the king's heart toward beneficent decrees; if the world is guilty [of misconduct], God tilts the king's heart toward evil decrees. Thus each and every decree that issues from the king's mouth originates from God; hence it is said, *He directs it to whatever He wishes* (Prov. 21:1).

To do what is righteous and just is more desired by the Lord than sacrifice (Prov. 21:3)—R. Eleazar, son of R. Simeon, said: Anyone who does what is righteous and just is accounted to God as though he had brought burnt offerings and sacrifices before Him, as it is said, *[It] is more desired by the Lord than sacrifice.* R. Jeremiah said: So long as there is righteousness and justice in the world, God is more pleased than He would have been with burnt offerings and sacrifices, as it is said, *[It] is more desired by the Lord than sacrifice.*[1]

R. Joḥanan said: When anyone dispenses righteous charity in secret, God diverts the angel of death—who is called Anger—from him and from the members of his household, as it is said, *A gift in secret subdues Anger, a present in private fierce rage* (Prov. 21:14). R. Levi said: The reward of him who gives it is greater than [the reward of] him who receives it. For he who gives it does so as an act of righteousness while he who receives it does not know whether it is proper for him to do so or not. For it is taught in a Mishnah: He who has fifty [zuz] and trades with them may not accept [charity]. And anyone who does not need to accept it yet accepts it nevertheless, such a one will not die of old age until he is driven [by necessity] to accept it from his fellow creatures. This is the general principle: Whosoever does not need to accept it yet accepts it nevertheless, will not depart from this world until he is driven [by necessity] to accept it from his fellow creatures. Conversely, anyone who is entitled to accept [charity], yet refrains from doing so, will not depart from this world until [he prospers enough] to dispense charity out of his wealth to others, as it is said, *Blessed is one who trusts in the Lord* (Jer. 17:7).[2]

He who strives to do right and kind deeds attains life, success, and honor (Prov. 21:21)—R. Eleazar, son of R. Simeon, said: Anyone who pursues righteousness will have children who are masters of Torah, masters of righteous charity, masters of [rabbinic] lore. Where [is the scriptural proof that they will be masters of] Torah? It is written here, *Life* (Prov. 21:21), and it is written elsewhere, *You shall have life* (Deut. 30:20).[3] Where [is the scriptural proof that they will be] masters of righteous charity? In the verse, *Attains life, success, and honor* (Prov. 21:21).[4] Where [is the scriptural proof that they will be] masters of [rabbinic] lore? It is written here, *Honor* (Prov. 21:21), and it is written elsewhere, *The wise shall obtain honor* (Prov. 3:35).[5]

One wise man prevailed over a city of warriors, and brought down its mighty stronghold (Prov. 21:22): *A city*—this refers to the heavens which are the city of the ministering angels; *One wise man prevailed*—this refers to Moses who scaled the heavens;[6] *and brought down its mighty stronghold*—this refers to the Torah. Where [in Scripture] are ministering angels called *mighty?* In the verse, *Bless the Lord, O His angels, mighty creatures who do His bidding* (Ps. 103:20). Where [is the scriptural proof that] Moses ascended on high? In the verse, *And Moses went up to God* (Exod. 19:3). Where [in Scripture] is the Torah called *stronghold?* In the verse, *May the Lord grant a stronghold to His people* (Ps. 29:11).

Another interpretation: *And Moses went up to God* (Exod. 19:3). R. Samuel bar Naḥmani said: Before the Torah was given, [we are told that] *The heavens belong to the Lord* (Ps. 115:16); these [the angels] could not descend [from heaven], nor could those [humans] ascend [to heaven]. Let me tell you a parable: To what may this be likened? To a king who, wishing to marry off his daughter, issued an interdict covering the Mediterranean basin. It said: "Romans may not go down to Syria, and Syrians may not go up to Rome." Once he married off his daughter he canceled the interdict.[7] So also, before the Torah was given from heaven, *The heavens belong to the Lord* (Ps. 115:16). Once the Torah was given, *Moses went up to God* (Exod. 19:3), and *The Lord came down upon Mount Sinai* (Exod. 19:20).

It is taught in the school of R. Ishmael: *Jethro, the priest of Midian,*[8] *heard* (Exod. 18:1). What did he hear [that caused him] to come?[9] R. Eliezer said: He heard about the war with Amalek and [as a result] came in [to become a proselyte], which is why the account [of this war] immediately precedes this verse.[10] R. Joshua said: When God wished to give the Torah to Israel, the entire world quaked. The [leaders of] all the nations of the world immediately gathered [to consult] Balaam, and asked him, "What is the meaning of the entire world quaking? Is God perhaps bringing another flood upon the world to destroy it?" He replied, "Benighted idiots that you are, [do you not know that] God has already sworn that He will not bring another flood and destroy the world, as it is said, *For this to Me is like the waters of Noah: as I swore that the waters of Noah nevermore would flood the earth, so I swore that I will not be angry with you or rebuke you* (Isa. 54:9)." They said, "Is he perhaps bringing a sheet of fire upon the world to destroy it?" He replied, "Neither a flood of water nor a sheet of fire. Rather [what causes the quaking is that] today He assumes kingship over the whole world, as it is said, *[The Lord sat enthroned at the Flood;] the Lord sits enthroned, king forever* (Ps. 29:10); He is giving the Torah to His people, as it is said, *May the Lord grant strength to His people; may the Lord bestow on His people well-being* (Ps. 29:11)." Then each and every one of them went back to his homeland.

He who guards his mouth and tongue, guards himself from trouble (Prov. 21:23)—R. Ishmael said: This shows that a person's death and resurrection are governed by his tongue. If he has earned merit and has kept his tongue, it quickens him; if not, it slays him, as David has said, *Death and life are in the power of the tongue* (Prov. 18:21).[11] Hence Solomon prophesied and added to the wisdom of his father, David, saying, *He who guards his mouth and tongue, guards himself from trouble* (Prov. 21:23).[12]

CHAPTER TWENTY-TWO

· · ·

A good name is preferable to great wealth, grace is better than silver and gold (Prov. 22:1): Come and see how precious a good name is in the world, for even if a person has a million gold denars but has not acquired a good name, he has acquired nothing, as it is said, *A good name is preferable to great wealth*. Likewise, even if a person has much silver and gold but has not acquired a name [for himself as a student] of Torah, he has acquired nothing, as it is said, *For they are a graceful wreath upon your head, a necklace about your throat* (Prov. 1:9). *Grace* (Prov. 22:1)—*grace* must refer to Torah, as it is said, *For I have given you graceful instruction; do not forsake my teaching* (Prov. 4:2), and it is also said, *My fruit is more graceful than gold, fine gold, and my produce better than choice silver* (Prov. 8:19).

The reward of humility is fear of the Lord, wealth, honor, and life (Prov. 22:4)—R. Ḥannin said: If a person merits acquiring humility and fear of the Lord, he will also merit acquiring *wealth, honor, and life*. If not, *Thorns and snares are in the path of the crooked* (Prov. 22:5); any one who is crafty *will keep far from them* (ibid.).

Train a child in the way he ought to go, he will not swerve from it even in old age (Prov. 22:6)—R. Eliezer [disagreed] with R. Joshua. R. Eliezer said, "If you educate your child in words of Torah while he is yet young, he will continually grow up according to them, as it is said, *He will not swerve from them even in old age*. It is like the tendril of a vine—if you do not train it when it is still [young and] moist, once it dries out you will be unable to do so."

R. Joshua said, "*Train a child in the way he ought to go*—why so?—*he will not swerve from it even in old age*. It is like an ox that has not been taught to plow [initially]; in the end it is too difficult to learn how."

Hence Scripture says, *If folly settles in the heart of a child* (Prov. 22:15). Who will remove it? R. Zebida said: The rod of the Torah will remove it from him, as it is said, *The rod of discipline will remove it from him* (ibid.). If one does not merit being of the tribe of moral instruction (*shebet musar*), then the rod of correction (*shebet musar*) will be [inevitably administered by] the royal

97

court. And that is what is meant by the proverb "A hint to the wise, a club to the fool."[1] If one merits it, he is of the tribe (*shebet*) of Torah, if not, he receives the rod (*shebet*) of the government [across his back]. It is taught in a Mishnah:[2] R. Neḥunya ben ha-Qaneh said: Whosoever takes upon himself the yoke of Torah is relieved of the yoke of the kingdom and of worldly ways. Whosoever throws off the yoke of Torah has the yoke of the kingdom and of worldly ways imposed upon him.

Incline your ear, and listen to the words of the sages; pay attention to my wisdom (Prov. 22:17): If you enter a house of study and see the sages sitting deeply engaged in their discussions of the Torah, incline thine ear to their words, in order that you be able to keep them, as it is said, *It is good that you store them inside you, and that all of them be constantly on your lips* (Prov. 22:18). Why so? *That you may put your trust in the Lord, I let you know today—yes, you* (Prov. 22:19)—Said Solomon: Today I have made my wisdom known in the world, so that it may be kept for generations.

Indeed, I wrote down for you excellent things (shalishim), wise counsel (Prov. 22:20)—Bar Huna said: This refers to counsels and knowledge of ages past, as it is said, *In time past (mitemol shilshom)* (Exod. 21:29); [or else it refers to the counsels and knowledge] of leaders, as you would say, *Captains over all of them* (Exod. 14:7).[3]

Another interpretation: *Excellent things (shalishim)* (Prov. 22:20)—R. Ishmael said: Every thing on that day [in which the Torah was given] came as a triplet (*meshullash*). Scripture is a triplet: Torah, Prophets, and Writings. The letters formed a triplet: alef, mem, taw,[4] [which together spell] *'emet* (truth). [Moses came] from a tribe that is third: Reuben, Simeon, Levi. [He was] one of three siblings: Moses, Aaron, Miriam. He was hidden for three [months]: *She hid him for three months* (Exod. 2:2). Israel is a triplet: priests, Levites, and Israelite commoners. It was the third month: *On the third new moon after the Israelites had gone forth from the land of Egypt, [on that very day, they entered the wilderness of Sinai* (Exod. 19:1), and there received the Torah]. R. Levi said: Thus you learn that every thing on that day came as a triplet, hence it is said, *Indeed, I wrote down for you a threefold lore,[5]* etc. (Prov. 22:20). This shows that by these triplets God taught Moses counsel and knowledge, gave them to him in truth, and wrote them for him in truth, so that he too might go and proclaim them to Israel in truth, as it is said, *To let you know truly reliable words, that you may give a faithful reply to him who sent you* (Prov. 22:21).

Do not rob the wretched because he is wretched, do not crush the poor in the gate (Prov. 22:22): Why does Solomon say *wretched* twice? [He meant that] such a one is wretched in life and wretched in possessions. Since he has no possessions, his wisdom is not heard, as it is said, *A poor man's wisdom is scorned, and his words are not heard* (Eccl. 9:16). He is also wretched in life because he has not a penny to live on, and so his [enjoyment of] life is stolen from this world.

Another interpretation: *Do not rob the wretched*—R. Aqiba said: The wretchedness of the poor is [difficult] enough [to bear without adding injustice], as the proverb puts it, "It is sufficient for the poor [that he is poor]—leave him to his poverty," [and do not add to his misery]. *Do not crush the poor* (ibid.)—R. Simon said: Have no pity on him at the time of judgment [in court]. Another interpretation: R. Aqiba said: One may not exercise mercy in judging.[6]

Another interpretation: *Do not rob the wretched because he is wretched*—R. Ḥiyya said: The poor are called by seven names, and these are: Poor, needy, afflicted, wretched, oppressed, destitute, downtrodden. Poor, as commonly understood. Needy (*ebyon*), for he yearns (*mit'awweh*) for all things—he sees food but cannot eat of it, he sees beverage but cannot drink of it. Afflicted, in that he is sparsely supplied with means of livelihood. Wretched, in that he is wretched in [material] possessions. Oppressed, for he is battered from place to place. Destitute, for he is crushed. Downtrodden, for he is pushed down to the lowest doorstep. Is all this poverty not enough, so that you must also rob him? Hence Solomon states explicitly in his Wisdom, *Do not rob the wretched because he is wretched, do not crush the poor in the gate.*

For the Lord will take up their cause, and despoil those who despoil them of life (Prov. 22:23)—R. Hamnuna said: *For the Lord will take up their cause*—in this world; *and despoil those who despoil them of life*—in the world to come.

Do not remove the ancient boundary stone that your ancestors set up (Prov. 22:28)—R. Simeon ben Yoḥai said: If you see a custom which your forefathers had introduced, do not disdain it—for example, Abraham who instituted the morning prayer, Isaac who instituted the afternoon prayer, or Jacob who instituted the evening prayer. You should not say, "I, too, will add another prayer," as it is said, *That your ancestors set up.*[7] What does *that your ancestors set up* mean? R. Joḥanan said: They set it not for themselves alone but for all subsequent generations.

See a man skilled at his work—He shall attend upon kings (Prov. 22:29)—Come and see the wisdom of Solomon who was diligent in doing God's work, for he built the Temple in seven years, although it took him thirteen years to build his own house.[8]

Another interpretation: *See a man skilled at his work*—when the Sanhedrin sought to include Solomon among the three kings and four commoners [to

whom the Mishnah denies a place in the world to come],⁹ the Shekinah stood
up before the Holy, praised be He,¹⁰ and said to Him, Master of both worlds,
have You ever seen anyone as diligent in doing Your work? And yet they wish
to count him among those consigned to [eternal] darkness! At that moment a
heavenly voice came forth, saying to them, *He shall attend upon kings; he shall
not attend upon those consigned to [eternal] darkness* (Prov. 22:29).

CHAPTER TWENTY-THREE

·   ·   ·

You see it, then it is gone (Prov. 23:5)—R. Ishmael said: There are three that returned to their place—Torah, Israel, silver and gold. Israel was beyond the River Euphrates, as it is said, *In olden times, your forefathers—Terah, father of Abraham and father of Nahor—lived beyond the River Euphrates* (Josh. 24:2). Where [is scriptural proof that] Israel returned to their place? In the verse, *They shall be brought to Babylon, and there they shall remain* (Jer. 27:22). Silver and gold came from Egypt, as it is said, *Each woman borrow from her neighbor [. . . objects of silver and gold and clothing]* (Exod. 3:22), *[The Israelites . . . borrowed from the Egyptians objects of silver and gold . . .] and thus they stripped the Egyptians* (Exod. 12:35–36). Where [is scriptural proof that the silver and gold] returned to their place? In the verse, *So Shishak king of Egypt [came up against Jerusalem, and took away the treasures . . . of gold]* (2 Chron. 12:9).

The Torah also came from heaven, as it is said, *From the heavens He let you hear His voice* (Deut. 4:36). But when they sinned in the incident of the golden calf, the [first set of] Tablets [of the Ten Commandments] were broken, and the words thereof flew back to their place, as it is said, *You see it, then it is gone.*[1]

R. Joḥanan said: Even though the Tablets broke, they were subsequently restored, as it is said, *Thereupon the Lord said to me, "Carve out two tablets of stone like the first"* (Deut. 10:1). All that was written on the first set of Tablets was written on the second, as it is said, *The Lord inscribed on the tablets the same text as on the first* (Deut. 10:4).

R. Eliezer asked R. Joshua,[2] "Master, when was the second set of Tablets given to Israel?"

R. Joshua replied, "On the Day of Atonement."

R. Eliezer asked, "Where is [your] proof of it?"

R. Joshua replied, "Just as it took forty days for the first set, so did it take forty days for the second set. Go and count from the day when the first set was shattered until the following Day of Atonement, and you will find it to be eighty days—forty and forty. [The first] forty Moses waited on earth, and [the second] forty he ascended to heaven and descended [again]."

R. Eliezer asked, "Master, what is the meaning of the verse, *You have sowed much and brought in little; you eat without being satisfied; you drink without getting your fill, you clothe yourselves, but no one gets warm; and who earns anything earns it for a leaky purse* (Hag. 1:6)?"

R. Joshua replied, "*You have sowed much and brought in little*—since the cessation of the ʿomer;[3] *you eat without being satisfied*—since the cessation of the showbread;[4] *you drink without getting your fill*—since the cessation of the libations;[5] *you clothe yourselves, but no one gets warm*—since the cessation of the garments of the High Priesthood;[6] *and he who earns anything . . .*—since the cessation of the shekel dues.[7]

Though the fig tree does not bud—since the cessation of the first-fruits,[8] *and no yield is on the vine*—since the cessation of water and wine libations;[9] *though the olive crop has failed*—since the cessation of the anointing oil and the oil of the [Temple] lamps,[10] *and the fields produce no grain*—since the cessation of the daily sacrifices and the additional sacrifices [for Sabbaths, festivals, and new moons];[11] *though sheep have vanished from the fold*—since the cessation of [all] sacrifices, *and no cattle are in the pen* (Hab. 3:17)—since the cessation of peace offerings.[12]

But what does Scripture say of the future, when the Temple shall be rebuilt? *The city shall be rebuilt on its mound, and the fortress in its proper place. From them shall issue thanksgiving and the sound of dancers* (Jer. 30:18–19). *My Lord God is my strength; He makes my feet like the deer's and lets me stride upon the heights* (Hab. 3:19).

The father of a righteous person will exault (Prov. 23:24)[13]—R. Ishmael said: Happy is David, king of Israel, who earned the merit of siring a wise son and of rejoicing in his wisdom; hence it is said, *He who begets a wise child will rejoice in him* (ibid.). What is said thereafter? *Your father and mother will rejoice; she who bore you will exault* (Prov. 23:25). R. Aqiba said: Even God and wisdom rejoiced in him, as it is said, *Your father*—this refers to God—*and mother*—this refers to wisdom, as it is written, *If you call to understanding and cry aloud to discernment* (Prov. 2:3).

Who cries, "Woe!" (oy), who, "Alas!" (awoy); Who has quarrels, who complaints; who has wounds without cause; who has bleary eyes? (Prov. 23:29)—R. Simeon said: Come and see how hard wine is [on a person], for there are thirteen "Woes" (*way*) said of it, and they are: *(Way-) Noah, the tiller of the soil, was the first to plant a vineyard. (Way-) He drank of the wine and (way-) became drunk, and (way-) he uncovered himself within his tent. (Way-) Ham, the father of Canaan, saw his father's nakedness and (way-) told his two brothers outside. But (way-) Shem and Japheth took a cloth, placed it against both their backs and, walking backward, they (way-) covered their father's nakedness; their faces were turned the other way, so that they did not see their father's nakedness. When Noah woke up from his wine, he (way-) learned what his youngest son had done to him* (Gen. 9:20–24).[14]

Solomon came [thereafter] and expounded this in his Wisdom: *Who cries, "Woe!" who, "Alas!":* [*Who cries, "Woe!"*]—woe to him who is a drunkard. *Who, "Alas!"*—woe to him and woe to his parents, as it is said, *If a man has a wayward and defiant son [. . . a glutton and a drunkard]* (Deut. 21:18–20). *Who has quarrels*—for once he is inebriated by his wine, he reveals secrets between one person and another, and [as a result] he *incites brothers to quarrel* (Prov. 6:19). *Who complaints* (Prov. 23:29)—for once he is inebriated by his wine, he rants excessively. *Who has wounds without cause*—for once he is inebriated by his wine, he goes and inflicts a wound [upon someone]. *Without cause*—why is this written? Because he has no just cause [to have done so]. *Who has bleary (ḥaklilut) eyes*—if a man earns the merit of drinking only as much as he needs, it tastes good to his palate (ḥikko). Accordingly, R. Ishmael expounded the verse, *His eyes are darker than wine* (Gen. 49:12), as meaning "give him wine that is pleasing to his palate." To whom is it pleasing? R. Eliezer says: To him who drinks only as much as he needs. R. Joshua says: To an elder, as it is said, *His teeth are whiter than milk* (Gen. 49:12). R. Jeremiah said: Read here not *teeth are whiter (leben shinayim)* but "to one of [ripe] years (le-ben shanim)." For just as milk pacifies an infant, so wine sets the mind of an elder to rest; hence it is said, *[His eyes are darker than wine] and one of [ripe] years* [will be pacified as an infant] *with milk*.

What is said thereafter? *Those whom wine keeps till the small hours, those who gather to drain the cups* (Prov. 23:30)—R. Eliezer said: Woe unto him who puts aside words of Torah but rises early for wine! What is said following that? *Do not ogle that red wine [as it lends its color to the cup]* (Prov. 23:31)—R. Joḥanan said: What is actually written (*ketib*) is *pocket (kis)*, but it is read (*qere*) *cup (kos)*—woe unto him who sets his eyes on the cup, for the [wine] seller sets his eyes on his pocket. What is said next? *In the end it bites like a snake; it spits (yaprish) like a basilisk* (Prov. 23:32)—just as the snake bites and kills, so does wine bite and kill; just as the basilisk separates (*maprish*) life from death, so does wine separate (*maprish*) life from death.[15]

CHAPTER TWENTY-FOUR

. . .

If you showed yourself slack in time of trouble, wanting in power (Prov. 24:10)—R. Abbahu said: Whoever is slack [in studying] words of Torah will have no power, nor will he be able to answer for himself in time of trouble.[1] R. Levi said: Whoever is slack in any way.[2]

These also are by the sages: It is not right to be partial in judgment (Prov. 24:23)—With this Solomon made wisdom known to the sages, so that they would not respect persons in [rendering] judgment. Why does Scripture say *not right?* How is it not right? If a wicked person who stands in a court of law happens to be wealthy and the judge shows favoritism because of it, all will curse him, saying, "Woe to this judge who has forfeited his life by showing favor to that person because he is wealthy," as it is said, *He who says to the guilty, "You are innocent," shall be cursed by peoples, damned by nations* (Prov. 24:24). If, however, the judge chastises that wicked man in judgment, he brings blessings of good things upon himself, as it is said, *But it shall go well with them who decide justly; blessings of good things will light upon them* (Prov. 24:25). What is said thereafter? *Giving a straightforward reply (nekoḥim) is like giving a kiss* (Prov. 24:26)—R. Levi said: This refers to words of reproof (tokaḥot), as it is said, *All are straightforward to the intelligent man, and right to those who have attained knowledge* (Prov. 8:9).

I passed by the field of a lazy man, by the vineyard of a man lacking sense (Prov. 24:30)—Just as with a field, if one does not plow it and plant it, it will be grown over with thorns and thistles; just as with a vineyard, if one does not hoe it and weed it, it will be grown over with weeds; so too the disciple of the sages, if he does not engage in the give-and-take of Torah study, in the end he will look for the beginning of a chapter and fail to find it, look for the beginning of a tractate and fail to find it, look for the beginning of a section and fail to find it.[3] *It was all grown over with thorns, its surface was covered with chickweed* (Prov. 24:31). R. Joḥanan said: This was because he breached the fence of Torah. But whenever words of Torah enter to find the chambers of one's heart vacant, they settle there and make themselves at home, and the inclination to Evil cannot prevail over them, nor can anyone dislodge them. A parable: To what may this matter be likened? To a king traveling in the wilderness who came across a dining hall and other chambers, all unoccupied. He forthwith entered and occupied them [so that no one could prevail over him nor dislodge him. So when words of Torah occupy the chambers of the heart], the inclination to Evil cannot prevail over them nor can anyone dislodge them.

CHAPTER TWENTY-FIVE

These too are proverbs of Solomon, which the men of King Hezekiah of Judah copied (Prov. 25:1). R. Levi said: By what merit did the men of King Hezekiah of Judah gain length of days? Because they were deliberate and evenhanded in judgment, as it is said, *Like golden apples in silver showpieces is a phrase well turned* (Prov. 25:11).

R. Ḥama bar R. Ḥanina said: What is meant by *These too* (Prov. 25:1)? It shows that [like Solomon] they were deliberate and evenhanded in judgment. For anyone who is short-tempered in judgment will in the end forget what he has to say. Thus we find that our teacher Moses, may he rest in peace, became short-tempered for a moment and forgot what he was to say, and Eleazar the priest had to answer in his stead, as it is said, *Eleazar the priest said to troops who had taken part in the fighting ["This is the ritual law that the Lord has enjoined upon Moses"]* (Num. 31:21)—meaning, "God commanded my teacher Moses, He did not command me [directly]."

Which the men of King Hezekiah of Judah copied (Prov. 25:1): Why was this said? I say that Proverbs, Song of Songs, and Ecclesiastes had been suppressed before they were made part of the scriptural canon! What is said in Proverbs [that made it seem offensive]? *She is bustling and restive; she is never at home. Now in the street, now in the square, she lurks at every corner* (Prov. 7:11–12). What is said in the Song of Songs? *My beloved to me is a bag of myrrh lodged between my breasts. My beloved to me is a spray of henna blooms* (Song 1:13–14). What is said in Ecclesiastes? *O youth, enjoy yourself while you are young! Let your heart lead you to enjoyment in the days of your youth. Follow the desires of your heart and the glances of your eyes—but know well that God will call you to account for all such things* (Eccl. 11:9).[1]

R. Joḥanan said: The sages wished to suppress Ecclesiastes because there were things in it that leaned toward heresy. They said, "Moses says, *Do not follow your heart* (Num. 15:39), whereas Solomon says, *Follow the desires of your heart and the glances of your eyes* (Eccl. 11:9)—the strap has been loosened,[2] as if there is neither justice nor Judge!" However, when they read further on *But know well that God will call you to account for all such things* (Eccl. 11:9), they admitted that Solomon had spoken well.

Another interpretation: *Which the men of King Hezekiah [of Judah] copied* (Prov. 25:1)—*copied (he͑tiqu)* must mean "interpreted," as it is said, *From there he moved on (wa-ya͑ateq) to the hill country* (Gen. 12:8), not to speak [of the verse], *Him who moves mountains without their knowing it, who overturns them in His anger* (Job. 9:5).[3]

Now this is a matter of reasoning from the minor to the major: if Moses, father of the prophets, father of the sages, father of prophecy, and father of wisdom, forgot what he was to say because he was short-tempered for a moment, how much more so does this apply to the rest of humanity! Ben Azzai said: If you take [too persistent] a stand about your own words, you will have rendered them invalid and will forget them.[4]

Like clouds, wind—but no rain—is one who boasts of gifts not given (Prov. 25:14)—R. Levi said: For the sin of those who make public pledges [to charity] but do not pay them, the heavens are stopped from shedding dew and rain. Why so? [The verse supplies the causal connection: *Like clouds, wind—but no rain* is caused by] *one who boasts of gifts not given.* God says, "Better for a person not to pledge than to pledge and not pay." For so did He make it explicit [elsewhere] at the hand of Solomon, king of Israel, saying, *It is better not to vow at all than to vow and not fulfill* (Eccl. 5:4).[5]

If you find honey, eat only what you need, lest, surfeiting yourself, you throw it up (Prov. 25:16). *If you find honey*—Rabbi [Judah the patriarch] said: This refers to Ben Azzai; *lest, surfeiting yourself, you throw it up*—refers to Ben Zoma.[6]

Like a club, a sword, a sharpened arrow, is a man who testifies falsely against his fellow (Prov. 25:18)—R. Abbahu said: Come and see how hard a thing informing [on someone to the authorities] is, that it is likened to these three things, spears,[7] sword, and arrows. Just as the spear pierces and kills, so does informing kill and slay; just as the sword kills and slays, so does informing kill and slay; just as the arrow is shot to kill, so does informing kill and slay. Just as David cursed [the informer], so did Solomon curse [the informer]: David said, *May the Lord cut off all flattering lips, every tongue that speaks arrogance* (Ps. 12:4); Solomon said, *Like a club, a sword, a sharpened arrow, is a man who testifies falsely against his fellow* (Prov. 25:18).

If your enemy is hungry, give him bread to eat; if he is thirsty, give him water to drink (Prov. 25:21)—R. Ḥama bar R. Ḥanina said: Even if he arises early to slay you, if he comes into your house hungry and thirsty, give him food and drink. Why so? *You will be heaping live coals on his head, and the Lord will reward you* (Prov. 25:22). Read not *will reward (yishalem)* you, but "will hand him over to you *(yashlimehu)."*

CHAPTER TWENTY-SIX

. . .

Do not answer a dullard in accord with his folly, else you will become like him (Prov. 26:4)—What is said thereafter? *Answer a dullard in accord with his folly, else he will think himself wise* (Prov. 26:5). R. Huna said: *Do not answer a dullard*—in a place where people know both you and him. Why so? *Else you will become like him*—so that people would not say, "Come and see this sage having give-and-take with that fool." R. Joshua ben Levi said: *Answer a dullard in accord with his folly*—in a place where people do not know either you or him. Why so? *Else he will think himself wise*—so that people would not say, "Were it not that this sage is suspect in the matters that the fool is speaking about, would he not remain silent?" As it is said, *Like a pebble in a heap of stones, so is paying honor to a dullard* (Prov. 26:8). R. Aleskandri[1] said: Anyone who pays honor to a fool is like one who casts a stone at a Mercurius.[2]

Like a madman scattering deadly firebrands and arrows (Prov. 26:18)— R. Eleazar ben R. Simeon said: [This refers to] anyone who continually casts aspersions on his colleague that are as hard as arrows, as it is said, *So is the one who cheats his neighbor, and says, "I was only joking"* (Prov. 26:19). What is written following it? *For lack of wood a fire goes out, and without a querulous man contention is stilled* (Prov. 26:20). Just as with fire, where there is no wood there is no fire, so where there is no evil gossip contention ceases. What is written following it? *Charcoal for embers and wood for a fire and a contentious man for kindling strife* (Prov. 26:21).

An enemy dissembles (yinnaker) with his speech, inwardly he harbors deceit (Prov. 26:24)—R. Ze'ira said: From a person's words you can tell *(hikker)* whether he is your friend or your enemy. For so we find that the evil Haman spoke [amicably] to Mordecai even while he hated him in his heart, as it is said, *Haman was filled with rage at Mordecai* (Est. 5:9). Likewise we find that the evil Esau spoke [amicably] to Isaac even while he hated him in his heart, as it is said, *And Esau said in his heart, "Let [but the mourning period of my father] come, [and I will kill my brother Jacob]"* (Gen. 27:41).

It is taught elsewhere: There are ten dotted passages in the Torah:[3]

The Lord decide between you and me (Gen. 16:5)—the second letter *yod* in *you* (*ubynyk*) is dotted, which indicates that what Sarah was saying was, "Let Hagar return to her status as handmaid."[4] Our father Abraham replied, "Once we have made her a matron, we cannot go back and enslave her," he explained, "for to do so would be a desecration of God's name; this being so, let God decide between your words and mine," as it is said, *[But God said to Abraham, "Do not be distressed over the boy or your slave;] whatever Sarah tells you, do as she says* (Gen. 21:12). Thus [the decision in] the former case about Hagar must have been the same in the latter case about Hagar.[5]

When his brothers had gone to pasture their father's flock (Gen. 37:12)— the particle *et*[6] is dotted, which indicates that they really went not to pasture [the flock] but to eat and drink. Now is this not a matter of reasoning from the minor to the major—if a lifesaver[7] came forth into the world when they went to eat and drink, how much the more so had they gone to study Torah?

Speak to the Israelite people, saying: When any of you or of your posterity who are defiled by a corpse or are on a long journey (Num. 9:10)—[*long* is dotted,] which indicates that even if one but steps outside of the doorstep of the Temple Court [on the fourteenth of Nisan, he is obligated to keep the Second Passover].[8]

He did not know when she lay down, or when she rose (Gen. 19:33). Why is [*rose*] dotted? To show that he was not aware of her lying down but was aware of her rising; that is to say he knew of the lying down of the elder and of the rising of the younger.[9] This teaches that one sin provokes another.

All the Levites who were recorded, whom at the Lord's command Moses and Aaron recorded by their clans (Num. 3:39)—[*Aaron*] is dotted, which indicates that Aaron himself was not included in the enumeration.

And one-tenth (*'issaron*) (Num. 29:15)—the letter *waw* in *one-tenth* (written *'isrwn*) is dotted, which shows that only one tithe was required and not two.[10]

When the Ark was to set out (Num. 10:35)—both before this and after it there are dots,[11] hence Rabbi [Judah the Patriarch] said: This was originally an entirely separate book, but [the rest of it] was suppressed.

We have wrought desolation at Nophah (Num. 21:30)—[*at*] is dotted,[12] which shows that they had left some survivors alive there.

Concealed acts concern the Lord our God (Deut. 29:28)—[*Concealed acts* is dotted,] which indicates that Israel said to God, "Master of the universe, [we accept the covenant given to us on condition that] we are commanded to observe what has been revealed to us, but not what is concealed." To which God replied, "You will not even be able to [fully] comprehend the revealed [parts of the covenant]!"

[Esau ran to greet him. He embraced him] and falling on his neck, he kissed him; and they wept (Gen. 33:4)—[*he kissed him*] is dotted, which shows that it was a kiss not of genuine love but one of hatred. R. Simeon ben Menasya said: How [indeed] was Esau considered at that moment, as one who loved or one who hated? [Obviously as one who hated,] as it is said, *Like channeled water is the mind of the king in the Lord's hand; [He directs it to whatever He wishes]* (Prov. 21:1). Thus you learn that the evil Esau spoke to Jacob while hating him in his heart, as it is said, [*One speaks to his neighbor in friendship,]* *but lays an ambush for him in his heart* (Jer. 9:7). R. Simon said: When Esau pleaded with his father Isaac, saying, *Bless me, too, Father* (Gen. 27:38), Isaac intended to bless him as he had blessed his brother Jacob. The holy spirit, however, immediately diverted him by saying to him, "Isaac, Isaac, have no faith in the pleadings of that wicked one," as it is said, *Though he be fair spoken, do not trust him; for seven abominations are in his mind* (Prov. 26:25).[13]

R. Joḥanan said: This shows that the holy spirit responded to Isaac, saying, "It is revealed and known before Me that Esau will destroy the Temple and enslave the twelve Tribes of Israel." Whereupon Jacob gave Esau an insignificant blessing, saying, *Yet by your sword you shall live, and you shall serve your brother* (Gen. 27:40). When [will Esau serve Israel]? So long as they sit and study the words of Torah. But if they transgress against the words of Torah, [as it is said,] *You shall break His yoke from your neck* (ibid.), then *the hands are the hands of Esau* (Gen. 27:22). If [Israel] merits it, *The voice is the voice of Jacob*, but if Israel does not, *the hands are the hands of Esau*.[14]

CHAPTER TWENTY-SEVEN

·   ·   ·

Let the mouth of another praise you, not yours, the lips of a stranger, not your own (Prov. 27:2)—R. Abba said: It is unseemly for a person to sing his own praises—[leave it to] *the lips of a stranger, not your own.*[1]

As iron sharpens iron so a man sharpens the wit of his friend (Prov. 27:17). *As iron sharpens iron*—this refers to Moses and the wicked Pharaoh who crossed words with each other. Another interpretation: *As iron sharpens iron*—this refers to Aaron's staff and the Egyptian magicians who vied with each other in making magic.

R. Zeʿira said: When Moses stood before the wicked Pharaoh, the latter asked him, "Who sent you?"

Moses replied, "*The Lord, the God of the Hebrews sent me to you* (Exod. 7:16)."

Pharaoh asked, "And what did He tell you?"

[Moses replied,] "*Let My people go, that they may worship Me* (Exod. 8:16)."

Pharaoh asked him, "Is there a god in the world with whom I am not familiar? *I do not know the Lord* (Exod. 5:2)." He went on to say, "By your life! Of all of the gods whom I know, each and every one of them sent me a letter, but this God whom you mention has never sent me a letter. However, wait a moment while I send for my chest where all royal letters are kept."

Whereupon Pharaoh sent [his servant] to fetch the chest as well as seventy scribes who knew [the] seventy languages [of the world], who began to read the letters before him. When he did not find God's name [in them] he said to Moses, "Did I not tell you so? *I do not know the Lord* (Exod. 5:2)."

Then Pharaoh sent for all the Egyptian magicians and said to them, "In all your days, did you ever hear of the God of these people?"

They replied, "Thus have we heard, that He is the son of the wise, the son of ancient kings is He," as it is said, *Utter fools are the nobles of Tanis; the sages of Pharaoh's advisers have made absurd predictions. How can you say to Pharaoh: "I am the son of the wise, the son of ancient kings"* (Isa. 19:11)?

God said to them, "You utter fools! You call yourselves wise and Me the son of the wise! By your lives, I shall exterminate your wisdom from the world," as it is said, *And the wisdom of its wise shall fail, and the prudence of its prudent shall vanish* (Isa. 29:14).

When Moses saw that Pharaoh was hardening his stand with words, he went back to the Almighty and said, "Master of the universe, did I not tell You at the outset, *Please, O Lord, make someone else your agent* (Exod. 4:13)? Now there is Pharaoh sitting and stabbing me with words, saying to me, *I do not know the Lord*" (Exod. 5:2).

God replied, "By your life! He said, *I do not know the Lord*—in the end he will know [Me]; he said, *nor will I let Israel go* (ibid.)—in the end he will let them go against his will."

Let me tell you a parable: To what may this matter be likened? To a king who said to his slave, "Go and bring me a fish from the market place." The slave went and brought him a rotten fish, whereupon the king said to him, "Here is my command: either eat the fish, or receive one hundred lashes, or pay a fine of one hundred *maneh*."[2] The slave said, "I will eat the fish," but before he had finished eating it [he changed his mind and] said, "I would rather receive one hundred lashes." By the time he received sixty or seventy lashes he said, "I would rather pay the hundred *maneh*." He thus ate of the fish, was lashed, and paid the [full] fine [thus suffering all three punishments].

So also did it happen to Egypt: they were lashed [with the plagues], [had to] let [Israel] go, and were relieved of their valuables [by the Israelites]. What caused them [all this trouble]? Their hardening themselves against God. Therefore He, too, dealt hard with them by the hand of Moses; hence it is said, *As iron sharpens iron* (Prov. 27:17).

He who tends a fig tree will enjoy its fruit, and he who cares for his master will be honored (Prov. 27:18)—R. Levi said: *He who tends a fig tree will enjoy its fruit*—if a person gains merit through [study of] Torah in this world, he shall eat the fruit thereof in the world to come. It is taught in a Mishnah: These are the things which have no measure: corner crop, [first fruits, the pilgrimage offering, almsgiving, and Torah study. These are the things of which a person eats the fruits in this world while the principal remains for him [to enjoy] in the world to come . . . and Torah study stands equal to them all].[3] Hence it is said, *He who tends a fig tree will enjoy its fruit, and he who cares for his master will be honored* (Prov. 27:18).

As face answers face in water, so the heart of man to man (Prov. 27:19)—R. Ḥanina said: Does water [really] have a face? Why then does Scripture say, *As face answers face in water?* Just as when you put water in a vessel and gaze at it, it seems as though the water has a face in it,⁴ *so the heart of man to man* [actually reflects what the seer has in his own heart].

Mind well the looks of your flock; pay attention to your herds (Prov. 27:23)—This refers to what Israel says in reply to God: "Master of all worlds, You know the state of Your flocks in this world; [we pray] *pay attention to Your herds* in the coming future." Where [in Scripture] is Israel called a flock? In the verse, *For you, My flock, flock that I tend, are men; and I, your shepherd, am your God* (Ezek. 34:31). And where [in Scripture] is Israel called herds? In the verse, *I will feed them in good grazing land, and the lofty hills [of Israel] shall be their pasture* (Ezek. 34:14).⁵ Just as the flock is pastured herd by herd, so shall Israel encamp [in the coming future] camp by camp, as it is said, *There, in the hills of Israel they shall lie down in a good pasture and shall feed on rich grazing land* (Ezek. 34:14).

CHAPTER TWENTY-EIGHT

．　．　．

Better a poor man who lives blamelessly—this refers to Jacob[1]—*than a rich man (ʿashir) whose ways are crooked* (Prov. 28:6)—this refers to the wicked Esau, as it is said, *Like a hairy (seʿar) mantle all over* (Gen. 25:25).

R. Huna said: Anyone to whom words of Torah are not dear, *his prayer is an abomination* (Prov. 28:9). R. Ḥannin said: Here it is said, *He who turns a deaf ear to instruction* (ibid.); while elsewhere it is said, *Who stops his ears* (Prov. 21:13), followed not by *to instruction* but by *at the cry of the wretched* (ibid.). Just as there [the conclusion is], *he too will call and not be answered* (ibid.); so likewise here [the conclusion is], *his prayer is an abomination*.

A rich man is clever in his own eyes, but a perceptive poor man can see through him (Prov. 28:11): *A rich man is clever in his own eyes*—this refers to the evil Haman—*but a perceptive poor man can see through him*—this refers to the righteous Mordecai. Another interpretation: *A rich man is clever in his own eyes*—this refers to the evil Pharaoh—*but a perceptive poor man sees through him*—this refers to Moses. Another interpretation: *A rich man is clever in his own eyes*—this refers to the evil Esau—*but a perceptive poor man sees through him*—this refers to Jacob.

He who covers up his faults will not succeed; he who confesses and gives them up will find mercy (Prov. 28:13)—R. Yudan said: He confesses in order to forsake them, as it is said, *Let the wicked give up his ways, the sinful man his plans* (Isa. 55:7).

He who tills his land will have food in plenty (Prov. 28:19)—If a person earns merit by study of Torah, *he will have food in plenty*, as it is said, *Come, eat of my food, and drink the wine that I have mixed* (Prov. 9:5). But he who *pursues vanities will have poverty in plenty* (Prov. 28:19), as it is said, *At scoffers He scoffs, but to the lowly He shows grace* (Prov. 3:34). It is taught in a Mishnah: If you have labored in Torah I have great reward [for you], but if you have been idle away from Torah [study], I have many idle [things] to raise against you.[2]

He who gives to the poor will not be in want, but he who shuts his eyes will be roundly cursed (Prov. 28:27)—R. Aqiba said: Anyone who gives alms to the poor *will not be in want,* but if he does not, *he who shuts his eyes will be roundly cursed.* He used to say: If a poor person comes to you in the morning, and you give him an *isar*³ and he goes on his way; and if then another comes at noontime, do not say to him, "I have already given to the first one." You are commanded to give also to the second, *since you don't know which is going to succeed, the one or the other, if both are equally good* (Eccles. 11:6).

CHAPTER TWENTY-NINE

. . .

By justice the king sustains the land, but a fraudulent man tears it down (Prov. 29:4)—R. Naḥman bar Isaac expounded this verse: If the judge resembles a king, who needs nothing [and is therefore not susceptible to bribery], *he sustains the land*; but if he resembles a priest, who makes the rounds of the threshing floors [in order to exact his priestly dues ahead of the other priests], *he is a fraudulent man [who] tears it down.*[1]

CHAPTER THIRTY

· · ·

The words of Agur son of Jakeh, [man of] Massa; the speech of the man to Ithiel, to Ithiel and Ucal (Prov. 30:1): *The words*—these are the words of Solomon; *Agur*—he who girded (ʿ*agur*) his loins for wisdom; *son of Jakeh* (*yaqeh*)—a son who is free (*naqi*) from all sin and transgressions; *Massa*—he bore (*nasa*) the yoke of God; *the speech of the man*—as the holy spirit rested upon him;[1] *to Ithiel* (*itiʾel*)—[so named] because he understood the letters of God (*otiyyotaw shel el*); or because he understood the signs (*otiyyotehen*) of the ministering angels; *and Ucal* (*ukal*)—[so named] because he could (*yakol*) stand by them.

How so? Because he ruled over the [heavenly] beings above and the [earthly] beings below. Where [in Scripture is there proof that he ruled over] the [heavenly] beings above? In the verse, *Solomon successfully took over the throne of the Lord*[2] *as king instead of his father David, and all went well with him. All Israel accepted him* (1 Chron. 29:23). And where [in Scripture is there proof that Solomon ruled] over the [earthly] beings below? In the verse, *For he controlled the whole region west of the Euphrates; from Tiphsah to Gaza, etc.* (1 Kings 5:4).

And yet, after all this kingship, and all this wisdom, and all this understanding, and all this praise, Solomon had to say, *I am brutish, less than a man* (Prov. 30:2)—unlike Noah, who was called "man," as it is said, *Noah was a righteous man, etc.* (Gen. 6:9)—*and have not the common sense of a man* (Prov. 30:2)—here *man* refers to Adam, as it is said, *The preparations of the heart are Adam's,*[3] *but what he says depends on the Lord* (Prov. 16:1).

Who has ascended heaven and come down? Who has gathered up the wind in the hollow of his hand? Who has wrapped the waters in his garment? Who has established all the extremities of the earth? What is his name or his son's name, if you know it? (Prov. 30:4):

Who has ascended heaven and come down?—Moses.
Who has gathered up the wind in the hollow of his hand?—Aaron.

Who has wrapped the waters in his garment?—Elijah.

Who has established all the extremities of the earth?—Our father Abraham.

What is his name?—His name is the Lord, as it is said, *The Lord, the Warrior—Lord is His name* (Exod. 15:3).

Or his son's name?—Israel, as it is said, *Israel is My firstborn son* (Exod. 4:22).⁴

Two things I ask of You; do not deny them to me before I die (Prov. 30:7). And they are these: *Keep lies and false words far from me; give me neither poverty nor riches, but provide me with my daily bread* (Prov. 30:8). Why so? *Lest, being sated, I renounce, saying, "Who is the Lord?" Or, being impoverished, I take to theft and profane the name of my God* (Prov. 30:9)—R. Levi said: How could it occur to you that Solomon was a liar, or a thief, or swore falsely [and thus profaned God's name]? Rather, you must say that he was [in fact] offering wise counsel to all future generations so they would not practice vanity.

R. Yudan said: These verses were spoken [by Solomon] only in order to impose greater stringency upon the words of Torah. There it is written, *You shall not swear falsely by the name of the Lord your God* (Exod. 20:7), but Solomon made it more stringent by saying, *Keep lies and false words far from me*. There it is written, *You shall not steal* (Exod. 20:13); but Solomon made it more stringent by saying, *Being impoverished, I take to theft and profane the name of my God*.

The leech has two daughters: "Give!" and "Give!" Three things are insatiable; four never say "Enough!" (Prov. 30:15). *The leech has two daughters: "Give!" and "Give!"*—why twice *"Give!"* and *"Give!"*? R. Simeon ben Yoḥai said: In the future Gehenna will cry out to God, "Give me the wicked, give me the wicked!"⁵

Three things are insatiable; [four never say "Enough!":] Sheol, a barren womb, earth that cannot get enough water (Prov. 30:15–16). And what is the fourth? *Fire which never says "Enough!"* (Prov. 30:16)—this is the fire of Gehenna which has no mercy on the wicked.

Three things are beyond me; four I cannot fathom: how an eagle makes its way over the sky; how a snake makes its way over a rock; how a ship makes its way through the high seas (Prov. 30:18–19). *How an eagle makes its way over the sky*—for no man knows its destination; *how a snake makes its way over a rock*—for no man knows its direction; *how a ship makes its way through the high seas*—for no man knows her way. The fourth thing: *How a man has his way with a maiden* (Prov. 30:19)—R. Joḥanan said: This refers to the rooster,⁶ for no man knows whence its seed shoots forth.

The earth shudders at three things, at four which it cannot bear—they are these—*a slave who becomes king; a scoundrel sated with food; a loathsome woman who gets married; a slave-girl who supplants her mistress* (Prov. 30:21–23)—R. Aleskandri said: Whence do we learn this? From [the story of] Hagar, Sarah's handmaid.[7]

Four are among the tiniest on earth, yet they are the wisest of the wise: they are these—*Ants are a folk without power, yet they prepare food for themselves in summer; the badger is a folk without strength, yet it makes its home in the rock; the locusts have no king, yet they all march forth in formation; you can catch the lizard in your hand, yet it is found in royal palaces* (Prov. 30:24–28). R. Jeremiah said: This refers to Edom, that wicked nation, for all that exists can be found there.[8]

There are three that are stately of stride, four that carry themselves well: they are these—*the lion is mightiest among the beasts.* Why so? *He recoils before none*—for he has no shame; *the greyhound, the he-goat, the king whom none dares resist* (Prov. 30:29–31)—just as the greyhound goes on its way without hesitation, so also an established kingship, against which you cannot stand.

If you have done foolishly in lifting yourself up, if you have been a schemer, then clap your hand to your mouth (Prov. 30:32)—Rabbah (some say R. Samuel bar Naḥmani) said: If a man [is willing to appear] foolish [in order to learn] words of Torah, in the end he will be lifted up; but *if you have been a schemer, then clap your hand to your mouth.*

Four that carry themselves well (Prov. 30:29):[9] they are these—*As milk under pressure produces butter, and a nose under pressure produces blood, so patience under pressure produces strife* (Prov. 30:33). R. Yannai expounded this verse: *As milk under pressure produces butter*—in whom do you find the butter of Torah? In him who expends all the milk that he suckled from his mother's breasts to produce [the butter of] his [learning in] Torah.[10] *A nose under pressure produces blood*—this refers to him whose master once chided him [unjustly] and who bore it in silence; such a one deserves to rule on whether a woman's bloody discharge is ritually unfit or fit.[11] *Patience under pressure produces strife*—this refers to him whose master had chided him [unjustly] more than once, and he bore it in silence; such a one deserves to rule on whether a case is a civil one or a capital one.[12]

CHAPTER THIRTY-ONE

· · ·

The words of Lemuel, king of Massa, with which his mother admonished him
(Prov. 31:1)—R. Joḥanan said: This shows that his mother hoisted him upon
the column [to whip him], and asked him, *"What, my son? and what, O son
of my womb? and what, O son of my vows? (Prov. 31:2)*—the son whom I
vowed to God; *do not give your strength to women, your vigor to those who
destroy kings* (Prov. 31:3)."

Why so? *Lest they drink and forget what has been ordained, and infringe
on the rights of the poor* (Prov. 31:5). What does *what has been ordained
(meḥuqqaq)* refer to? R. Simon said: It refers to the words of Torah, as it is
said, *Inscribed (ḥaquqim) on both their surfaces* (Exod. 32:15).

Another interpretation: *Massa* (literally, "the burden") *with which his
mother admonished him* (Prov. 31:1)—R. Ishmael said: On the same night that
Solomon completed the labor of [building] the Temple, he wed the daughter of
Pharaoh so that the rejoicing over [the completion of] the Temple and the rejoicing over Solomon's wedding to the daughter of Pharaoh were held concur-
rently, the sound of the latter drowning out the sound of the former, for as the
proverb puts it, "Everyone flatters the king."[1] It was just then that the thought
came to God's mind that some time in the future He would destroy the Temple,
as it is said, *This city has aroused My anger and My wrath from the day it was
built until this day* (Jer. 32:31).

R. Levi said: [God's anger was also caused] by the fact that [on the following morning] the daily burnt offering was offered as late as the fourth hour of
the day. How did this happen? Bithiah, the daughter of Pharaoh, made a kind
of canopy to which she affixed images of all kinds of stars and constellations,
and she hung it over his wedding couch. Every time that Solomon wanted to
arise, he saw all these stars and constellations [hanging over him and thought
it was still nighttime,] so that he slept on until the fourth hour of the day.[2] R.
Levi said: That was the very day when the daily burnt offering was offered at
the fourth hour.

What a rare find is a capable wife! Her worth is far beyond that of rubies

(Prov. 31:10): [*What a rare find is a capable wife!*]—this refers to the Torah. *Her worth is far beyond that of rubies (peninim)*—for she had been [kept] in the Innermost (*lifnai lifnim*) [Chamber],³ and Moses earned the merit of bringing her down to Israel. *Her husband puts his confidence in her, and lacks no good thing* (Prov. 31:11)—for no good thing is lacking in her [the Torah].

Another interpretation: *What a rare find is a capable wife!*—a tale is told of R. Meir that while he was sitting and expounding in the academy on a Sabbath afternoon his two sons died.⁴ What did their mother do? She left them both lying on their couch and spread a sheet over them.

At the close of the Sabbath, R. Meir came home from the academy, and he asked her, "Where are my two sons?"

She replied, "They went to the academy."

He said, "I looked for them at the academy but did not see them."

She [silently] handed him the cup [of wine] for the Habdalah Benediction,⁵ and he pronounced it. Then he asked her again, "Where are my two sons?"

She replied, "Sometimes they go someplace (*maqom*)⁶ [first]; they will be back presently." She served him [his meal] and he ate. After he recited the Grace after meals she said to him, "Master, I have a question to ask you."

He replied, "Ask your question."

She said, "Master, some time ago a certain man came by and left something on deposit with me. Now he has come to reclaim this deposit. Shall I return it to him or not?"

He replied, "My daughter, is not one who holds a deposit obligated to return it to its owner?"⁷

She said, "Without your opinion [on the matter] I would not give it back to him."

What did she do [then]? She took him by the hand, led him up to the children's room, brought him to the bed, and removed the sheet, so that R. Meir saw them both lying on the bed dead. He burst into tears, saying, "My sons, my sons! My masters, my masters! My natural born sons, and my masters who enlightened (*me'irin*) me with their [learning in] Torah."

At this point R. Meir's wife said to him, "Master, did you not just now tell me that we must return a pledge to its owner?"

To which he replied, *The Lord has given, and the Lord has taken away; blessed be the name of the Lord* (Job 1:21). R. Ḥanina said: In this manner she comforted him and brought him solace, hence it is said, *What a rare find is a capable wife!* (Prov. 31:10).

R. Ḥama bar R. Ḥanina said: Of what were R. Meir's two sons guilty that they both died at the same time? It was because they used to leave the academy and sit around eating and drinking. R. Joḥanan said: Indeed [one may be judged guilty] even for mere idleness. For when God gave the Torah to Israel, the one thing with which He charged them was [the duty to study] words of Torah, as it is said, *The Lord your God commands you this day to deserve these laws and rules* (Deut. 26:16).

She is like merchant fleet, bringing her food (laḥmah) from afar (Prov. 31:14)—R. Simeon ben Ḥalfota said: If one is not willing to expose himself [fully] to words of Torah, he will never learn it, for *food* [here actually] refers to Torah, as it is said, *Come, eat my food (laḥmi), and drink the wine that I have mixed* (Prov. 9:5).

She rises while it is still night, and supplies provisions for her household, the daily fare of her maids (Prov. 31:15)—so long as a disciple of the wise sits and studies Torah by night, God draws a thread of lovingkindness about him by day, as it is said, *By day may the Lord vouchsafe His lovingkindness, [so that at] night a song to Him may be with me, a prayer to the God of my life* (Ps. 42:9). Not only that, but God will also provide his daily food, as it is said, *And supplies provisions for her household* (Prov. 31:15).

Now food (*teref*) here means sustenance,[8] as it is said, *He gives food (teref) to those who fear Him* (Ps. 111:5), and it says, *The dove came back to him toward evening, and there in its bill was an olive-leaf (teref) as food;*[9] then *[Noah] knew* (Gen. 8:11). [What did Noah know?] Happy is he whose sustenance is bitter like the [unripe] olive yet given to him by the hand of God, rather than sweet as honey but given to him by the hand of flesh-and-blood. Why so? For God feeds and sustains all of his creatures, as it is said, *You give openhandedly, feeding every creature to its heart's content* (Ps. 145:16).

Many women have done well, but you surpass them all (Prov. 31:29)— Adam was commanded six commandments;[10] Noah was commanded [not to eat] a limb from a live animal; Abraham was given the commandment of circumcision, and Isaac was accordingly circumcised on the eighth day; Jacob [was given the commandment] prohibiting [the eating of] the sciatic nerve; and Judah was given the commandment obligating a levir to marry his deceased brother's childless widow. But you were given the 248 positive commandments, corresponding to the 248 members [of the human body], and each and every member says to the person [of whom it is a part], "I beseech you, perform this [my] commandment with me." You were also given the 365 negative commandments, corresponding to the days of the solar year, and each and every day says to the person, "I beseech you, do not commit this transgression on my day."

Grace is deceptive, beauty is illusory; it is for her fear of the Lord that a woman is to be praised (Prov. 31:30): *Grace is deceptive*—the grace of Noah was deceptive, even though it is said, *But Noah found grace with the Lord*

(Gen. 6:8), for as R. Levi explained, only in his generation [was he considered a good man].[11] *Beauty is illusory*—Adam's beauty was illusory, for as R. Simeon ben Menasya said, the heel of Adam's foot shone so bright that it eclipsed the sun. Now do not marvel [at this statement]. As is the way of the world, when a person makes two salvers, one for himself and one for a member of his household, whose does he make more beautiful? Not his own? Even so Adam was created to serve God, while the sun was created for the use of [God's] creatures. Is it not even more logical, then, that if his heel had eclipsed the sun, the radiance of his face should have eclipsed it even more so?

It is for her fear of the Lord that a woman is to be praised (Prov. 31:30)—this refers to Moses.[12]

Of all women, *It is for her fear of the Lord that a woman is to be praised. Extol her for the fruit of her hand, and let her works praise her in the gates* (Prov. 31:30–31)—R. Jose bar Jeremiah said: Why are the prophets likened here to women? Because, just as such a woman is not embarrassed to demand the needs of her household from her husband, so were the prophets not shy about demanding Israel's needs from God. God said to Israel, "My children, study Torah day and night, and I shall account it to you as though you had established the entire universe, as it is said, *Let not this book of the Torah cease from your lips, [but recite it day and night]* (Josh. 1:8);[13] *I charge you: Be strong and resolute* (Josh. 1:9); *Praise the Lord; for He is good, His steadfast love is eternal* (Ps. 136:1); *All the people raised a great shout extolling the Lord, because the foundation of the house of the Lord had been laid* (Ezra 3:11); *Buy truth, and never sell it, and wisdom, discipline, and understanding* (Prov. 23:23); *They will be yours alone, others having no part with you* (Prov. 5:17); *Instruct a wise man, and he will grow wiser; teach a righteous man, and he will gain in learning* (Prov. 9:9); *For through me your days will increase, and years be added to your life* (Prov. 9:11).

NOTES

·　·　·

INTRODUCTION

1. This is not the place to provide a general introduction to midrashic literature. The reader is referred to the many excellent introductions already published, including Joseph Heinemann, "Preaching in the Talmudic Period," *Encyclopaedia Judaica* 13 (Jerusalem: Keter, 1972), 994–98; Moshe David Herr, "Aggadah," *Encyclopaedia Judaica* 2, 354–64; Herr, "Midrash," *Encyclopaedia Judaica* 11, 1507–14; Samuel Horowitz, "Midrash," *Jewish Encyclopedia* 8 (New York: Funk and Wagnalls, 1904), 548–50; Julius Theodor, "Midrash Haggadah," *Jewish Encyclopedia* 8, 550–69; Shalom Spiegel, Introduction to *Legends of the Bible* by Louis Ginzberg (Philadelphia: Jewish Publication Society, 1956); James Kugel, "Two Introductions to the Midrash," *Prooftexts* 3 (1983), 131–55; Barry Holtz, "Midrash," in *Back to the Sources,* ed. Barry Holtz (New York: Summit Books, 1984), 177–212; and Burton L. Visotzky, *Reading the Book: Making the Bible a Timeless Text* (New York: Anchor/Doubleday, 1991).

2. For this distinction see R. E. Brown, *The Birth of the Messiah* (New York: Doubleday, Image Books, 1979), app. 8, "Midrash as a Literary Genre," 557–63.

3. For a bibliography of introductory materials to MM see Burton L. Visotzky, "Midrash Mishle" (Ph.D. diss., Jewish Theological Seminary of America, New York, 1983).

4. See especially chaps. 6–8.

5. See the translation and notes to chap. 10, ad loc.

6. See, e.g., Gershom Scholem, *Major Trends in Jewish Mysticism* (New York: Schocken Books, 1946), 71; M. S. Cohen, *The Shiʿur Qomah: Liturgy and Theurgy in Pre-Kabbalistic Jewish Mysticism* (Lanham, Md.: University Press of America, 1983), 57–59.

7. The issue, however, is much more complicated. Although the literary sources lead to the conclusion that this was a Palestinian custom (Louis Ginzberg, *A Commentary to the Palestinian Talmud,* 4 vols. [New York: Jewish Theological Seminary, 1941], 4:144; Z. M. Rabinowitz, *Ginze Midrash* [Tel Aviv: Tel Aviv University Press, 1976], 237, n. 36; B. M. Lewin, *Osar Ḥilluf Minhagim* [Jerusalem: Mosad Harav Kook, 1942], 101), archeological evidence points to doubled doors also in virtually all of the contemporary synagogues in the diaspora. See chap. 8, n. 21.

8. See MM (ed. Visotzky, 1983), 47–48 nn. 106–07, and the commentary there to chap. 1, lines 41–42.

9. It is not entirely clear from the mention in MM chap. 1 whether twenty years is required for any leader in prayer or only for those who pronounce the priestly benediction. See the notes to the text for more detail and bibliography.

10. Daniel al-Qumisi's commentary to Mic. 5:12, and Hos. 3:4, in I. D. Markon, ed., *Pitron Shnem 'Asar* (Jerusalem: Mikze Nirdamim, 1957), 5, 46.

11. A. Marmorstein, "Fragments of the Commentaries of the Karaite Daniel al-Qumisi," *Hazofeh* 9 (1925) 136.

12. Salo Baron, *A Social and Religious History of the Jews,* 18 vols. (New York and Philadelphia: Columbia University Press and Jewish Publication Society, 1958), 8: 26, 32.

13. See the notes throughout, and especially my cross-references to the Hebrew critical edition. For the insignificance of the issue see Adolf Neubauer, "Review of 'Midrash on the Proverbs,' Critically Edited with a Commentary and Detailed Preface by Salomon Buber," *Jewish Quarterly Review* 6 (1894), 165.

14. See *The Midrash on Psalms,* trans. William Braude (*YJS 13*) (New Haven: Yale University Press, 1959), xxv. For Haggadat Mishle see Nathan's *'Aruk* (G. A. Kohut, *Aruch Completum* [New York: American Academy for Jewish Research, 1923]), s.v. "*naqad,*" 3; and *Mahzor Vitry,* ed. Horowitz (Nuremburg, 1923), p. 684 and cf. p. 55. The printed editions of *Mahzor Vitry* are based, however, on fourteenth-century manuscripts, so the traditions of this work may be reliably dated only to that era, three hundred years after its composition.

15. Nahmanides at the end of his commentary to the Torah; Roqeah, *Hilkot Shabbat* no. 55; Mordekhai on B. BM, chap. 3, no. 253.

16. *The Fathers According to Rabbi Nathan,* trans. Judah Goldin (*YJS 10*) (New Haven: Yale University Press, 1955), xxi.

17. Introduction, *Midrash Bereshit Rabbati,* ed. Chanoch Albeck (Jerusalem: Mosad Harav Kook, 1940), 28.

18. See Cohen, *Shi'ur Qomah,* 51–65.

19. *Ginze Kedem,* 5:57, and cf. Lewin, *Osar Hilluf Minhagim,* 100–01.

CHAPTER ONE

1. This is a technical term with a broad range of meaning, e.g., he opened his discourse, or the eyes and ears of his listeners, or the hidden meaning of the verse. Cf. Luke 24:31–32, 45. See further Joseph Heinemann, "The Proem in the Aggadic Midrashim," *Scripta Hierosolymitana* 22 (Jerusalem: Magnes Press, 1971), 100–22.

2. In YSh Prov. 929 this is brought as an explanation of the oversized letter *mem* (the numerical value of which is forty) in the first word of the book of Proverbs, *mishle*. On the idea of Solomon's fasting, see Dov Noy, *Motif Index of Talmudic-Midrashic Literature* (Bloomington: Indiana University, 1954), no. 523 and Louis Ginzberg, *Legends of the Jews,* 7 vols. (Philadelphia: Jewish Publication Society, 1909–1938) 6:282 n. 18.

3. Here, and throughout MM, I translate a variety of abbreviations of rabbinic epithets for God with the simple English appellation. For more on the literal meanings of the Hebrew terms see the Introduction.

4. For this motif see Noy, *Motif Index,* no. 512. See also PR 14(59a) and YSh Kings 173.

5. This prooftext is followed by a brief excursus on the relation of wisdom to Torah, which assumes that knowledge is a prerequisite for Torah. This is supported by the interpretation of Ps. 111:10 as a statement of precedence: first comes wisdom, then Torah. Finally, the excursus recalls Solomon's choice of wisdom over all else and credits him with being like his father, David (conveniently omitting the latter half of 1 Kings 3:3 which refers to Solomon's offerings at the forbidden high places).

6. Literally, "there they teach" (Ab 3:18).

7. Referring back to the quotation from 2 Chr. 1:12.

8. Given by God because of Solomon's special merit. Similar use of the term is found regarding Moses, Aaron, and Miriam, and the gifts given them because of their merit in B. Ta 9a.

9. See the contrasting definitions in Sifre Deut. 13, ed. Louis Finkelstein (Berlin: Gesellschaft zur Förderung der Wissenschaft des Judenthums, 1939; reprinted New York, 1969), 22.

10. I have added 1 Kings 5:10 to provide what is otherwise an understood link between this homily and the following text.

11. Note well that in 1 Kings 5:11, Solomon is made out to be wiser than Adam, yet in Prov. 30:2, Solomon modestly claims Adam to be wiser than himself.

12. There is a play here on "Ezrahite" and "one from the East" (*mi-mizrah*). The proof is based on the notion that this verse refers to Abraham (the Isaiah passage is the prophetic lesson for Gen. 12). A fanciful tale based on this same interpretation is told about Nahum of Gimzo in B. Ta 21a. The entire paragraph here is taken from PesDRK Parah 3, Lev. Rabbah 9:2.

13. Other versions of this Queen of Sheba legend may be found in Midrash HaHefes and the Second Targum to Esther 1:3, 8–10. See the discussions by Solomon Schechter, "Queen of Sheba Legends," *FolkLore* 1 (1890), 349–58; Ginzberg, *Legends of the Jews,* 6:290, nn. 42, 43, 46 and 4:145–47; and A. Wünsche, *Bibliotheca Rabbinica* (Leipzig: Otto Schulze, 1885), viii. For the motif see Noy, *Motif Index,* no. 490.

14. Or perhaps, "Proverbs."

15. Cf. Gen. 41:16.

16. This riddle is found in Aramaic in Lam. Rabbah 1:11. See Noy, *Motif Index,* no. 496.

17. Cf. Neg 9:3 and 11:7, where this phrase is applied to one who confirms the words of the sages.

18. This combination of riddle with incestuous relationship recalls the Oedipus cycle. See Noy, *Motif Index,* no. 498. Cf. Ker 3:5–6.

19. Cf. Gen. 19:30–38. Lot fathered both his daughters and his grandchildren. He was therefore his daughters' incestuous husband, and the daughters were their children's sisters by the same father.

20. There is no biblical evidence that Solomon had eunuchs at his court, although Samuel had predicted that the kings of Israel would employ them (1 Sam. 8:15). Here they probably represent the type of Oriental court that would have

received the Queen of Sheba, and the local customs of royalty in the Levant during the ninth century. Parched grain and nuts are a treat for children (B. Pes 109a).

21. Literally "took in their clothing."

22. The Ark was the locus of God's presence, the Shekinah. Rabbanite Jews of the ninth century bowed in this way as a mark of respect for the Scrolls of the Torah housed in the synagogal arks.

23. See Ginzberg, *Legends of the Jews* 5:234 n. 131, and 6:290 n. 43.

24. See *Torah Shelemah* to Gen. 17:3, no. 30, and Targum Jonathan to Num. 24:4.

25. Balaam and Job and friends are counted among the Gentile prophets—men with access to the Shekinah. See Ginzberg, *Legends of the Jews* 6:125 n. 727.

26. This is an old debate, dating back to Plato and Aristotle; see *Oxford Classical Dictionary,* 2d ed., s.v. "anatomy."

27. This statement is probably a gloss, and the prooftexts should be taken as support of R. Joshua's contention rather than as support of Solomon's agreement with the opinion R. Joshua would hold centuries later. The parallelism in the verse seems to imply that "glad" and "wise" are equivalent in meaning.

28. Cf. *Otiyyot de-Rabbi Aqiba,* under the letter *lamed.*

29. Ps. 1:1 begins with *alef,* the first letter of the Hebrew alphabet. Ps. 150:6 begins with the eleventh letter of the twenty-two-letter Hebrew alphabet, *kaf.*

30. Prov. 1:1 begins with the thirteenth letter of the Hebrew alphabet, *mem* (see above, n. 2). Prov. 31:31 begins with the last letter, *taw.* Heart (*leb*) begins with the letter *lamed,* the twelfth letter of the Hebrew alphabet. The idea of picking up where one's predecessor left off is also found in MT 1:5 and GenR (pp. 1228, 1296).

31. See Ginzberg, *Legends of the Jews* 6:283 n. 24.

32. The verse beginning in the middle of the alphabet; see above, n. 30.

33. Inferential reasoning was one of the intellectual qualities cultivated in the rabbinic academies. Cf. B. Shab 31a, Sanh 93b, Hag 14a.

34. R. Joshua takes the verse as a question followed by an imperative response: Do you wish to receive tradition (*laqaḥat musar*)? Then be discerning (*haskel*)!

35. Here, too, the verse is seen as question and response: Do you wish to receive ethical instruction (*laqaḥat musar*)? Then be just (*ṣedaq*)!

36. The simplest qualification for a fit judge. See Sifre Deut. 144 (p. 199), and for more qualifications B. Sanh 7b.

37. Literally, "the world," here and later in this sentence.

38. Cf. B. BB 8b. Rashi to B. Shab 33a, which explains that corrupt judgment occurs when the judge does not deliberate long enough to be precise.

39. The same word (*mesharim*) rendered as *equity* in the biblical verse.

40. Just as the judge exerts himself to give correct judgment, so will the angels exert themselves to bring him his reward, measure for measure.

41. Cf. 1 Kings 3:7.

42. Twenty is often considered the age of majority in rabbinic literature. See Nid 5:9, B. Shab 89b, B. BB 121b, P. Bik 2:1 (64c), *Torah Shelemah* to Gen. 3:22, no. 202, and to Gen. 23:1, 32: 3, with the commentaries ad loc. See the discussion in Viktor Aptowitzer, *Kain und Abel* (Vienna: Löwit, 1922), 97–99, n. 7. Twenty was apparently considered the age of majority by the Karaite Daniel al-Qumisi (S.

Poznanski, "Daniel ben Moses al-Kumisi," *Jewish Encyclopedia* 4, 432–34; *Karaite Anthology*, trans. Leon Nemoy [*YJS* 7] [New Haven: Yale University Press, 1952], 31) and by the Qumran sectarians (L. Schiffman, "The Eschatological Community of the *Serekh Ha-'Edah*," *Proceedings of the American Academy for Jewish Research* 51 [1984], 110–21).

43. These two prooftexts from Numbers are difficult—one would have expected one verse that mentions both the age of twenty and service; unfortunately no such verse is found in the Hebrew Bible or in the versions. Num. 4:47 mentions thirty years (supporting R. Aqiba), and the Septuagint Greek version of that verse reads twenty-five years (supporting R. Meir). In any case, it is odd to find R. Ishmael debating R. Meir, who was his junior. Cf. B. Ḥul 24a, where the age of service is debated as to whether it is twenty-five or thirty. In B. ʿAr 11a the verse is taken to refer to the age for Levitical singing, and this interpretation gives rise to the opinion of Resh Laqish which follows: that the topic of debate relates to the appropriate age for leading synagogue services. See Saul Lieberman, *Tosefta Ki-fshuṭah* (*TK*) (New York: Jewish Theological Seminary of America, 1962), Ḥag, p. 1276 (and see n. 42 above for reference to the Qumran community's interpretation of the verse). The substitution of synagogue worship for Temple service was a major tenet of rabbinic theology following the Temple's destruction; cf., for example, B. Ta 2a.

44. This is an allusion to the two bodies of knowledge, Torah and wisdom. If one masters wisdom (*yishmaʿ ḥakam*), he also gains in Torah (*leqaḥ*). For the equation of Torah with learning (*leqaḥ*), see 4:2.

45. Another play on words: as a reward for seeking rabbinic instruction (*taḥbulot*), he is granted portions (*ḥabilot*) in this world and the next.

46. *Ḥidotam*, derived from the root *ḥwd* (literally, "to obscure, to tie in a knot"), hence the inference "bind them."

47. Cf. MT 104:3, B. ʿAZ 19b, Suk 21b.

48. See Ginzberg, *Legends of the Jews* 6:285 n. 27.

49. Literally, "there we recite." Most often this phrase is used by Palestinian sages to refer to the Mishnah, although in later Midrashim it may refer to other Tannaitic statements (see J. N. Epstein, *Mabo le-Nusaḥ Ha-Mishnah*, 2d ed. [Jerusalem: Dvir, 1964], 888–91). This particular quotation is not in our text of the Mishnah; cf. Abot de-Rabbi Nathan, ed. Solomon Schechter (Vienna, 1887; reprinted with corrections, New York: Feldheim, 1967), chap. 24, p. 78; and Seder Eliahu Zuta, ed. Meir Friedmann (Vienna: Wahrmann, 1904; reprinted Jerusalem, 1969), chap. 16, p. 8. See also Sifre Deut. 48 (108–09), 188 (277); Midrash Tannaim, p. 4; and Midrash hag-Gadol Deut., ed. Solomon Fisch (Jerusalem: Mossad Bialik, 1972), 228–29.

50. Ab 4:6; the Mishnah goes on: Anyone who profanes the Torah, he himself is profaned by others.

51. Only constant repetition enables the sage to recall instantly the chapters and tractates of the Oral Law.

52. Even if a written Scroll is before him, the sage still must rely on his memory to find the beginning and end of a passage in the unpunctuated text.

53. When a father teaches his child Torah it is as if the child had personally received it at Mount Sinai (B. Qid 30a).

54. These terms—*fit, unfit, forbidden, permitted*—constitute the main tools

of the rabbi's trade. The Nazirite and the anointed priest are also commanded to be very sensitive to these rulings, for they are forbidden to contact ritual unfitness. The Torah gives the reason for each of them: *And the priest . . . shall not become unfit . . . for the crown of the anointing oil of God is upon him* (Lev. 21:10–12); *All the days of his vow of Naziriteship . . . he shall not become unfit . . . for the crown of God is upon his head* (Num. 6:5–7). These verses explain why Torah will serve as a crown.

55. See Samuel Krauss, *Griechische und Lateinische Lehnwörter im Talmud und Midrasch* (Berlin: S. Calvary, 1899; Hildesheim: Olms, 1964), s.v. *"qtl̲."*

56. When the throat is opened to give voice to words of Torah, the words become a necklace, as above. The connection is followed into Song 4:9, *Thou hast ravished my heart . . . with one bead of thy necklace.* The necklace of Torah is alternately described as milk and honey in Song 4:11.

57. Prof. H. Z. Dimitrovsky pointed out in a personal communication that at first glance it is odd to find David quoting Proverbs, a work that the sages attributed to his son, Solomon. The solution to this puzzle is found in 13:1—*A wise son is instructed of his father*—which Prof. Dimitrovsky assumes refers to Solomon. Hence, in Proverbs 13 Solomon is merely repeating what he had heard from David, his father.

58. Cf. James 2:10–11.

59. Sanh 4:5.

60. The prooftext is based on a wordplay: "stored up" (*ṣofenin*) is paired with *let us lie in wait* (*niṣpenah*). The verse is then understood in the sense that those who lie in wait for blood will have their sins stored up against them, while the innocent (*naqi*) will have a clean slate (*ḥinnom*).

61. Cf. Gen. 37:19–20 and Tanḥuma Buber Wa-yesheb 13 on these verses.

62. The verse begins, *Let us set an ambush to shed blood.* Hence God refers to the blood which they conspire to spill. *The innocent* is taken to refer to Joseph.

63. The biblical phrase quoted is attributed to Judah in the Bible. The error is probably due to the author or to a scribe quoting from memory; cf. Gen. 37:22.

64. A play: "His innocence" (*tummo*) is paired with *whole* (*temimim*).

65. The proof comes as well from the preceding verse, *Simeon and Levi are brethren.* GenR 99:7 comments, "Brothers to Dinah, but not to Joseph whom they sold." *Their council* (*be-sodam*) is understood here as "their secret," viz., that they put Joseph in the pit.

66. See GenR 84:19, where this disagreement is reported in the names of R. Eliezer and R. Joshua.

67. As eldest son, Reuben cared for Jacob's household; see Julius Theodor's commentary to Genesis Rabbah, 2d ed. (Jerusalem: Wahrmann Books, 1965) 84:15 (p. 1018).

68. In penitence for the incident with Bilhah. See Gen. 35:22 and Sifre Deut. 31 (p. 52).

69. See Gen. 15:13 for the decree that Israel is to go down to Egypt. God provided them with a sustainer, Joseph (Gen. 45:5).

70. See Gen. 44:8. This may refer to the Israelites' despoliation of Egypt at the Exodus (see Exod. 12:35).

71. This aside on the ten martyrs represents a very popular theme in the Middle

Ages. See the hymn entitled *Elah Ezkerah* recited in the supplementary prayer of the Day of Atonement. This martyrology is tied to medieval mystical circles by M. D. Herr, "The Ten Martyrs," *Encyclopaedia Judaica* 15, cols. 1006–08. In part, the translation here follows Saul Lieberman, *Greek in Jewish Palestine* (New York: Jewish Theological Seminary, 1942), 196 n. 21.

72. Joseph used the chalice as a divining cup; see Gen. 44:5. For the term *chalice*, see Krauss, *Lehnwörter,* s.v. "*klyd.*" In addition to casting lots, the purse (*kis*) is taken to be the cup (*kos*). Cf. Prov. 23:31 and Lev. Rabbah 12:1.

73. This clause is found in all but one manuscript of MM.

74. Cf. Gen. 43:32 and Targum Jonathan ad loc.

75. The verse is usually translated, *And on the crown of the head of the prince among his brothers. Nazir* may mean "Nazirite" or "wearer of the princely crown."

76. Literally "the narrow-eyed one." Cf. B. Sotah 38b.

77. The nets are spread with food to attract the birds. See Rashi on this verse.

78. A play: *their own blood* (*damam*) and "cash" (*damim*).

79. Those who inform on others for personal gain. See Saul Lieberman, *Hellenism in Jewish Palestine* (New York: Jewish Theological Seminary, 1950), 191–93. The remainder of this paragraph, concluding with the prooftext from Job 12:6, is obscure and perhaps was garbled by the scribes.

80. B. BQ 119a.

81. "Explicating" (*mefaresh*) may also mean "sails upon the sea."

82. The duplication *she speaks out* (*amareha to'mer*) leads to the conclusion that the same independent judgment must be given in either of the two instances, rich or poor. For the pronouncement of judgment see Sanh 3:7.

83. Following the translation of Lieberman, *Hellenism,* 200 n. 5. When Moses promulgated Deuteronomy he informed Israel that it was on God's authority (the *spirit* in 1:23) that he spoke. See Sifre Deut. 5 (p. 13).

84. See Sifra Be-ḥuqqotay, 112c.

85. See Deut. 4:36.

86. See Zech. 7:7, which led the author to assume this prooftext was spoken by Jeremiah.

87. In the manuscripts and parallels (e.g., LevR 26:8, B. Yoma 77b) to this passage the amount of time varies from two and a half to as many as six and a half years.

88. I translate *ki* as in Aramaic, "when, until."

89. Cf. Jer. 15:15–21.

CHAPTER TWO

1. For the idea that performance of the commandments will save Israel from suffering, cf. *Mekhilta,* ed. Saul Horowitz and Israel Rabin (Frankfurt am Main: Wahrmann, 1928–31, reprint ed., Jerusalem, 1970) Be-shallaḥ, 169–70; B. Shab 118a; Sanh 98b; and *Menorat Ha-Ma'or,* 4 vols., ed. H. Enelow (New York: Bloch, 1929) 3:222. The war of Gog and Magog is the "last terrible battle with the enemies of God" (Solomon Schechter, *Aspects of Rabbinic Theology* [New York: Macmillan, 1909], 102). The pangs of the Messiah are the birth pangs that accompany the advent of the world to come. For the torment of Gehenna see MM above, on 1:6.

I translate *din* as "torment" following Saul Lieberman, *Texts and Studies* (New York: KTAV, 1974) 18 n. 80.

2. Ab 4:14, following the translation in H. Danby, *The Mishnah* (Oxford: Oxford University Press, 1938), ad loc.

3. This paragraph is a condensation of Tos Hor 2:7 (see Saul Lieberman, *Tosefet Rishonim,* 4 vols. [Jerusalem: Wahrmann, 1939] 2:202). The worthless person referred to here is the son of the unlearned (*'am ha-'areṣ*, see B. BM 85a). The comparison of the teacher of such a one with God is also in MT 116:8.

4. The dialogue between these two colleagues, here represented as disciple and teacher, is problematic. See Y. L. Zunz, *Ha-Derashot be-Yisrae'el,* ed. Chanoch Albeck (Jerusalem: Mossad Bialik, 1947), 133, 412 n. 78.

5. MM here may be referring to the legend that the infant in utero knows Torah; see B. Nid 30b.

6. *Sound wisdom* is Torah. See PRE 3, Deut. Rabbah 1:19, and Tan. Lek Lekah 11. On the protective power of Torah see B. Sot 21a, Qid 82a, and Ket 77b.

7. A play on the word *mesharim,* which may mean "straight road" and "straight conduct, righteous behavior." The literal meaning here is that the words of Torah will be made a straight road before him, so that he will understand them correctly and apply them properly. For vindication of the innocent and indictment of the guilty, see B. Sanh 6b.

8. "*Good* refers to Torah" is a very common association of ideas. See below, chap. 21; B. Ber 5a, 48b, etc.

9. Ab 4:10, cf. Danby, *Mishnah,* ad loc.

10. A very common midrash; see below at 6:22, Ab 6:9, Sifre Deut. 34, B. Sotah 21a, etc.

11. Cf. Exod. 32:15.

12. "Torah" here refers to the giving of the Ten Commandments, as above. See Exod. 20:1–14. The order of the two prooftexts is mistakenly reversed in the Hebrew text. See below to 5:2 for another interpretation of the two-edged sword. Other versions of this discussion on the meaning of the two-edged sword are found in PesDRK (p. 207) and parallels.

13. MM provides no comment on Prov. 2:13–4:22.

CHAPTER FOUR

1. Cf. Tos Pe'ah 1:2, where the evil tongue is likened to spilling of blood, to idolatry, and to illicit sexual intercourse.

CHAPTER FIVE

1. See Prov. 7:5–10, where the forbidden woman and the promiscuous woman are equated.

2. See above, chap. 2, n. 4.

3. Cf. above, chap. 2 at nn. 10–11.

4. The term for "glory" (*hod*) is the same one for "vigor" in Prov. 5:9.

5. "Ruthless angels" (*'akzarin*) is paired with the strangers (*another* [*zarim*]) of Prov. 5:10.

6. This pairs *your toil* (*'asabeka*) in 5:10 with *'asab*, "to be sad, to regret." Cf. Gen. 6:6, *And the Lord regretted that He had made man on earth, and His heart was saddened (wa-yit'asseb).*

7. That is, the fountain (*meqor*) of Torah and the source (*meqor*) of his livelihood.

8. For Torah as a *loving doe,* cf. MT 119:41.

9. Study of Torah is likened to suckling at the breast in Sifre Deut. 321 (p. 370) and in B. 'Er 54b.

10. The motif of the sinner thinking that he can hide from God is found in reference to the adulterer (Tos. Sot 3:5, Num. Rabbah 9:9) and the thief (B. BQ 79b).

11. This idea is contrary to the reading in the modern printed editions of B. Qid 40a, where humanity is given the benefit of the doubt—intention to fulfill a commandment is credited whereas intention to commit a sin is not. However, the text here is supported by the reading in old editions of B. Qid and in manuscripts of the Tosefta upon which the homilist here was drawing. See Lieberman, *TK* Pe'ah, p. 127.

12. Ab 2:1, following Danby's translation.

13. Women in childbirth are in mortal danger; hence they must recite the deathbed confession. See B. Shab 32a.

14. When tormented in Gehennah, one is informed of the reasons for his punishment—his iniquities.

CHAPTER SIX

1. *Stranger (another)* is taken to represent the "strange worship" of idolatry.

2. Cf. Deut. 32:1 and Isa. 51:6.

3. This odd English translation renders the equally odd Hebrew expression; the meaning is, of course, "showed preference for good deeds."

4. Here the pun is *zar (stranger)* and *akzari* ("cruel").

5. Cf. B. Ber 56a; exile atones for sin. Here, the midrash discusses foreign rule over the land of Israel.

6. *The power of your fellow* being the merit of Torah study performed by the patriarchs.

7. The atoning power of Torah is detailed in Sif Deut. 306 (p. 337) and B. Sot 21a.

8. Ab 4:11.

9. That is, fast. Cf. Ta 2:1.

10. See below, to Prov. 6:5.

11. Hebrew *qabbalah,* literally "tradition" as received and transmitted. The term is used in Rabbinic literature to denote the last two sections of the biblical canon, the Prophets and Hagiographa. For further information see S. Leiman, *The Canonization of Hebrew Scripture* (Hamden, Conn.: Connecticut Academy of Arts and Sciences, 1976), 572 n. 278.

12. Cf. B. Yoma 86a.

13. Many kinds of food preparation are forbidden on the Sabbath (see Shab 7:2), so it is necessary to prepare the Sabbath meal in advance, usually on Friday

afternoon before sunset. For the analogy cf. B. ʿAZ 3a, Eccles. Rabbah 1:15, Pes. Rabbati 198b.

14. Cf. Ab 4:16. For the relation of the rooms and their functions in the Graeco-Roman world see Petronius, *Satyricon,* trans. William Arrowsmith (Ann Arbor: University of Michigan, 1959), 27–28.

15. "Summer and winter," lit. "days of sun and days of rain."

16. This is an interpolation into God's tirade against sinners. On the two Rabbis and their relationship, see above, on Prov. 2:7.

17. Perhaps *slumber* is connected with the morning benediction, "Praised be You . . . who has removed the bands of sleep from my eyes and slumber from my eyelids" (B. Ber 60b).

18. *Hugging* (lit. "folding hands") refers to foreplay. *In bed* (*lishkab*), lit. "to lie," is used in both biblical and rabbinic Hebrew to mean sexual intercourse.

19. *Mehallek* ("calling") is paired with *melek* ("king"), and *resheka* ("poverty") is paired with *roshka* ("your head").

20. These activities are assumed to be signals by which the informer betrays his victims to the authorities. Cf. Matt. 26:48–49 and parallels.

21. Note that this list contains seven items. The rabbis take the fact that the verse says first six and then seven to mean that the sum total should be thirteen. Hence they enumerate a second list not mentioned in Proverbs. For another solution to this textual difficulty see Midrash Tannaim to Deut. 22:19 (p. 140).

22. Lit. "uncovering the nakedness." Cf. Lev. 18:6–23.

23. The tongue of the gossip or informer.

24. Cf. B. Pes 113b, where the Soncino Talmud translates the term as "lecherous old man."

25. On the institution of flatterers in antiquity see B. Sot 41b and Athenaeus, *Deipnosophists,* trans. Charles Gulick (London: Heinemann, 1929), 6:248c–262b.

26. This is a popular rabbinic maxim. The scribe inserted here the entire statement about plagiarism, including the scriptural prooftext.

27. See above, to Prov. 2:11.

28. Usually this refers to the Mishnah, but it may also refer to some nonmishnaic Tannaitic source (see Epstein, *Mabo,* 888–91). The text here is cited in Enelow, *Menorat Ha-Maʾor* 3:228, in the name of R. Meir, mentioned below. But cf. Sif Num. 41 (p. 44), where a similar homily appears which also is quoted in Midrash Ḥakamim in Rabbi Judah the Patriarch's name.

29. Added from the MSS and parallels.

30. Presumably all who have too much knowledge are here identified with those who have smooth alien tongues. The idea here is obscure.

31. Elisha ben Abuyah was one of the great scholars of his generation and a teacher to R. Meir. Elisha sinned (see below, n. 39) and was exiled from the rabbinic community. Nevertheless R. Meir continued to study with him, and although Elisha no longer observed Jewish law, he took pains to assure that his disciple, Meir, continued to observe. Meir maintained his loyalty to his master throughout his lifetime.

32. Other manuscripts read "and has cast shame upon his Torah," instead of the rhetorical question we have here. A *ḥaber* is a table-fellow who was trusted by the rabbis to maintain the strictest degree of ritual fitness (viz., that required of the

priesthood to be allowed to eat sacrificial meat during Temple times). Such a person had to be thoroughly learned in all the details of rabbinic observance.

33. This paragraph is a parenthetical commentary on Prov. 6:26 and interrupts the narrative about R. Meir and R. Elisha ben Abuyah.

34. The Torah prescribes death for the adulterer and the adulteress (Lev. 20:10). The question here seems to be: Granted that the adulterer receives the death penalty in this world, how may he earn the right to resurrection in the world to come?

35. Since both verses use the term *unpunished,* the hermeneutic device of analogy based on verbal congruity leads to the conclusion that they refer to the same principle (See Lieberman, *Hellenism,* 58–62 for more on this device). The merits that the sinner forfeits might otherwise have earned him a place in the world to come.

36. I find no parallel for this odd prescription. It seems to be a case of measure for measure: the adulterer departed from the Torah and left his own child fatherless, hence he is required to raise another's child in the way of Torah.

37. There is no atonement without repentance. See Yoma 8:8.

38. Lit. "the principal essence."

39. Rabbinic tradition is unclear about the exact nature of Elisha's sins. Cf. B. Hag 14b–15b and P. Hag 2:1 (77b).

40. First the teacher would read the unvocalized and unpunctuated text, then the student would repeat it correctly.

41. A slip of the tongue interchanging the two liquids, *l* and *r*. This interchange of liquid sounds was common in both the Hebrew and the Greek of the period.

42. Elisha takes this as an omen. See Lieberman, *Hellenism,* 194–99.

43. Latin *speculator* (a term also taken over into the Greek language), a soldier "employed in carrying messages, and seeking out those who were proscribed or sentenced to death" (Liddel and Scott, *A Greek-English Lexicon* [Oxford: Clarendon Press, 1968], s.v.). See Samuel Krauss, *Lehnwörter,* s.v. *spykwlʾ* and Bauer, Arndt, Gingrich, and Danker, *Greek-English Lexicon of the New Testament and Other Early Christian Literature* (Chicago: Univ. of Chicago Press, 1957), s.v.

44. Lit. "lay down." There is a play on the words *kibbah* ("extinguished") and *shakebah* ("lay down") here and in Ruth 3:13.

45. The Hebrew *mador* may mean either "compartment" or "fireplace." The number fourteen is derived from *sevenfold* (Prov. 6:31), which could be understood as twice seven.

46. *Devoid of sense* (Prov. 6:32)—lit., "lacketh heart."

47. Wisdom is visible in the radiance of one's face. See P. Shab 8:1 (11a), B. Ned 49b, Eccles. Rabbah 8:1, *Tanḥuma* (ed. Buber [Vilna, 1885]), Ḥuqqat 17, 18.

48. This concluding sentence leads directly into the next chapter, as happens also at the end of chapters 7, 10, and 17. MM provides no comment to Prov. 7:1–24.

CHAPTER SEVEN

1. See above, chap. 6, n. 48.

CHAPTER EIGHT

1. This verse is first understood in the context of the commentary on Proverbs chap. 7: If you call upon wisdom, then understanding will put forth her voice (viz., answer you). In the subsequent commentary, however, the verse is taken as it has been translated in the body of the text.

2. This term has mystical overtones. See Visotzky, MM (diss.), 74 n. 19.

3. "Chanting" here renders the same Hebrew word used for *shouts* in Prov. 8:3.

4. The idea that the patriarchs observed the Torah, while it is an obvious anachronism, is a commonplace in rabbinic literature.

5. See Gen. 3.

6. See Dan. 9:21, where the ministering angel Gabriel is called *ish* (man).

7. See Ps. 82:7.

8. Unfit and fit, forbidden and permitted are the basic categories of things in Jewish law.

9. Lit. "the chamber of chambers," i.e., God's throne chamber. See n. 2 above. Some texts add, "and also hidden things which are in the depths," but this seems to be an extraneous gloss and is omitted in a number of MSS.

10. Perhaps referring to Sif Deut. 37 (p. 70). Cf. Gen. Rabbah 1:4 (p. 6), where there is a full list of parallels. The list varies from text to text. B. Pes 54a, B. Ned 39b, and PRE chap. 3 are closest to the list here.

11. Here and below, words in the prooftexts indicating antiquity are presumed to refer to the time before creation.

12. Usually translated *eastward*.

13. Usually translated *May his name be continued as long as the sun*. The word for *be continued, yinnon,* is taken as a proper name in B. Sanh 98b.

14. Usually the author asks, "What *follows* this verse?" He has taken an earlier tradition on the seven things created before the world (see above, n. 10) and inserted it here by virtue of its connection with the Torah. Although Torah is first in the list of seven, the prooftext for Torah is cited last, for it links the paragraph with Prov. 8:22. Thereafter, however, he makes use of another earlier tradition (see below, n. 15) based on Prov. 8:21; hence he asks rhetorically, "What is written just before it" [i.e., before Prov. 8:22].

15. *Substance* (*yesh*) has the numerical value of 310 (10 [*yod*] + 300 [*shin*]), according to the hermeneutic device called *gematria*. This very popular tradition is found in some editions of ʿUq 3:12 (cf. Epstein, *Mabo,* 979), B. Sanh 100a, and elsewhere.

16. This motif is found also below, to Prov. 31:10. Moses is the gnostic revealer who brings pristine knowledge to earth in order to save humanity.

17. This tradition is found in a variety of forms in rabbinic literature. ARN (B) chap. 43 (p. 19) is the closest to our text, citing the same ten names. I have followed J. Goldin's translation of the first seven names in ARN (A) chap. 37 (Goldin, *YJS 10,* 154; Schechter, *ARN,* 110). For a list of seven earths, see Lev. Rabbah 29:11 and PRK RH (p. 344); of four earths, Gen. Rabbah 13:12, MhG Gen. 2:7; of seven lands, PRE 18, and below, to Prov. 9:1; of six lands, Song Rabbah 6:4 and Esther Rabbah 1.

18. 'Arqa (the Aramaic synonym of the Hebrew 'ereṣ, "land") is paired with 'areq (in the mind of the author) and then translated into the Hebrew bareḥah ("fled").

19. The opening word of Genesis is be-reshit (in the beginning).

20. A weak pun: gay ("valley") is paired with givʿah ("hill").

21. See the discussion and sources cited by Rabinowitz, Ginze Midrash, 237 n. 36; and by T. Friedman, "Some Unexplained Features of Ancient Synagogues," Conservative Judaism 36 (1983), p. 38 nn. 33–37. Friedman's point that diaspora synagogues had a forecourt is well illustrated in Sardis, Priene, Ostia, Dura, Delos, Aegina, Naro, and Stobi—virtually every diaspora synagogue so far uncovered. Louis Ginzberg's explanation (Commentary to the Palestinian Talmud [New York: Jewish Theological Seminary, 1941] 4:144) of this passage needs revision, and the custom cited here is not indicative of any specific provenance of MM.

22. Ishmael's opinion is found in Sif Deut. 36 (p. 66), Midrash Tannaim 29, and B. Men 34a. The disagreement mentioned here is not found elsewhere.

23. Hebrew nefesh can mean both "soul" and "self."

CHAPTER NINE

1. For more on the seven firmaments or heavens see Ginzberg, Legends, 5:10 n. 22.

2. That is, the original seven lands that form the Land of Israel. Cf. Josh. 3:10. The earth as a whole, however, is divided into sevenths; see Ginzberg, Legends 5:12 n. 28.

3. This is a popular tradition; similar versions of it are found in P. Meg 1:7 (70d), etc. See Ginzberg, Legends 6:481 n. 194.

4. Joshua was R. Aqiba's disciple. Cf. B. ʿEr 21b.

5. Elijah the prophet, who frequently appeared to the Rabbis. See M. Friedmann's introduction to SER, 2–44. For Elijah as a priest, see Ginzberg, Legends 6:316 n. 3.

6. See Lev. 21:1ff.

7. Those who were slain during the Hadrianic persecutions, when conducting burials was forbidden by the Roman authorities under pain of death. See Tosafot to B. BM 114b, Yeb 61a.

8. The four-arched gate (Greek: tetrapylon) of Caesarea has elicited a considerable amount of discussion. See most recently Daniel Sperber, "Greek and Latin Words in Rabbinic Literature: Prolegomena to a New Dictionary," Bar Ilan Annual, 14–5 (1977), 37–38.

9. Cf. the description of Elisha's room in 2 Kings 4:10, and Ginzberg, Legends 6:329 n. 62.

10. For the import of this term see Lieberman, Greek in Jewish Palestine, 77.

11. Of Yavneh. See Visotzky, MM (diss.), 282 n.

12. See Noah's curse on Canaan in Gen. 9:25.

13. See Gen. 18:2.

14. See Lev. 16:16–17.

15. This poem is found first in Mek Be-shallaḥ (p. 141) and later in many other Midrashim.

16. Ab 2:4. See Epstein, *Mabo,* 1182 and the variant readings in Visotzky, MM (diss.), 287 for the authorship of this passage.

17. The point of the parable appears to be that until the sage shares his wisdom by teaching others, God cannot be pleased with his learning.

18. Ab 4:10, also quoted above, chap. 2.

19. Seemingly a jibe at the Christian doctrine of original sin.

20. Lit. "stole the mind of"; refers to *stolen waters* in Prov. 9:17.

21. *Her guests* (lit. "those whom she calls") is read as "they call out." For the watchers, cf. B. Ber. 60b (top) and Rashi's commentary ad loc.

22. See chap. 6, n. 48.

CHAPTER TEN

1. Cf. B. Shab 156b and BB 10a.

2. An apparent contradiction in the same scriptural phrase, usually translated "[God] will by no means clear the guilty"; the literal translation is "clearing, He will not clear." Here the phrase is split into two phrases, "He will clear" and "He will not clear."

3. Cf. Mek Yitro ba-Ḥodesh (pp. 227–28) and parallels.

4. Mek ibid.; Tos Kippurim 4(5):8 (p. 252) (and see Lieberman, *TK,* 824–25); B. Yoma 86a; P. Yoma 8:8 (45b); Sanh 10:1 (27c); Sheb 1:9 (33b); and ARN (A) chap. 29 (Goldin, *YJS 10,* 121–22).

5. See chap. 2 n. 4.

6. The atoning power of the Land of Israel is also discussed in the comment on Prov. 17:1. Cf. Sif Deut. 333 (p. 383).

7. This is part of a theodicy explaining why the righteous suffer in this world. Cf. Buber, *Tanḥuma,* Introduction and p. 131, where MS Oxford reads, "Happy are the righteous, for God punishes them while they are still alive."

8. That is, to his reward in the world to come.

9. Literally, "order it."

10. See below for the examination given by God on Judgment Day.

11. R. Simon suggests that in addition to the reward in the world to come, the righteous do not suffer want in this world. This is in opposition to the view suggested above.

12. Guaranteeing them their punishment and cutting off the possibility of God's mercy intervening in their behalf.

13. A common rabbinic epithet for God.

14. See Joel 4:2. The name of the valley means "valley [called] 'God judges.'"

15. Cf. B. Sanh 7a.

16. The verb "read" refers to scriptural studies, while "recited" refers to Oral Torah or Rabbinics.

17. See SER chap. 1 (p. 4); E. E. Urbach, "On the Question of the Language and Sources of the Book *Seder Eliahu,*" (Hebrew) *Leshonenu* 21 (1956–57), 190; and idem, "Traditions about Merkabah Mysticism in the Tannaitic Period," *Studies in Mysticism and Religion Presented to Gershom G. Scholem* (Jerusalem: Magnes Press, 1967), 25–27. For the term "well grasped," see B. MK 28a, Pes 50a.

18. B. BB 75a.

19. MM and SER (cited above) expound this verse: *In the morning*—that is, on Judgment Day; *shall you hear my voice*—in an examination about my studies; . . . *will I order*—arrange the Oral Law that I have learned (see n. 9 above); . . . *will look forward*—in mystical speculation (see below).

20. This is the beginning of a series of progressively more difficult and esoteric subjects—a rabbanite curriculum. See, for a comparable curriculum, B. BM 33a; Shab 31a; Suk 28a; ARN (A) chap. 13; ARN (B) chap. 28; SEZ chap. 1 (p. 167). The combination here, Scripture but no Mishnah, probably refers to the Karaites. See SER chap. 15 (p. 70) and chap. 16 (p. 72); and SEZ chap. 2 (p. 171).

21. Cf. Zeph. 3:3.

22. Out of the six orders of the Mishnah. Cf. Sif Deut. 306 (p. 339, l. 4).

23. The ascending order of the curriculum indicates that the term "recite" refers to the midrashic commentaries on these biblical Books and not to the biblical Books themselves. This is now confirmed by a fragment of this passage from the Cairo Geniza (TS-AS 74, 2), which explicitly names the midrashic commentaries by their rabbinic titles.

24. See Lev. 11.

25. See Lev. 13.

26. See Lev. 13.

27. See Lev. 14.

28. See Lev. 15.

29. See Lev. 12.

30. See Lev. 13.

31. See Lev. 16:21.

32. A rabbinic hermeneutic device discussed in the introduction to the Midrash on Leviticus entitled Sifra (or Torat Kohanim). See Lieberman, *Hellenism*, 61, for more on this device.

33. See Lev. 27.

34. "Rule" and "instituted" have the same Hebrew root.

35. See above, n. 23, and the use of the term *ḥumshin* in B. Qid 33a (and Rashi's comment ad loc.).

36. See Num. 15:38.

37. This list may refer to items of disagreement between the Rabbanites and the Karaites. See Encyclopedia Judaica 10, 781 and Moses Zucker, *'Al Targum Rav Saadiah Gaon LaTorah* (New York: Feldheim, 1959), 203 n. 794. Cf., however, Lev. Rabbah 22:1 (ed. Margulies [Jerusalem: Wahrmann, 1972], 496, and the editor's comment ad loc.).

38. This is the congregational response in the *Qaddish*, the rabbinic doxology recited following a sage's discourse. The text of the response here is in Hebrew, although some of the manuscripts and the liturgy have it in Aramaic. Cf. Sif Deut. 306 (p. 342), B. Shab 119b, and Ber 57a.

39. See Sefer Hekalot (3 Enoch), passim; and the English translation and commentary by P. Alexander in the *Old Testament Pseudepigrapha*, vol. 1, ed. J. H. Charlesworth (New York: Doubleday, 1983), 223–315. On the subject in general see Gershom Scholem, *Major Trends in Jewish Mysticism* (New York: Schocken Books, 1946) 71. For the term "glory" see Hekalot Rabbati, in *Bet HaMidrash*, 6 vols. ed. Adolph Jellinek (Leipzig, 1853–77; reprinted Jerusalem, 1967) 3:83–108,

chap. 10; and M. Idel, "The Place of Torah in the Hekalot Literature," (Hebrew) *Meḥqere Yerushalayim Be-Maḥshebet Yisra'el* 1 (1981), 31 n. 30.

40. A string of verbs with similar meanings, such as this, is often found in the mystical literature. It becomes a chant, or mantra, which enables the mystic to enter the realm of his speculation. See Idel, ibid., p. 35 n. 36 and p. 36 nn. 37–38.

41. Cf. Ezek. 1:5ff.

42. Cf. Ezek. 1:4, 1:27.

43. Cf. Ezek. 1:14.

44. This planet plays a substantial role in later Franco-German mysticism. Some texts read "cherub" instead. For the latter reading, cf. Ezek. 10.

45. Rigyon is the stream that flows beneath God's throne. It is identified with the fiery river of Dan. 7:9–10. Cf. Hekalot Rabbati, chap. 13. For more on the river see Martin S. Cohen, *The Shi'ur Qomah* (Lanham, Md., 1983), 241 n. 12.

46. For the phrases round and square, but referring to sweets (figs), see Ter 4:8.

47. *Ofanim,* a class of angels. See Ezek. 1:16, 10:13.

48. *Gilgalim,* another class of angels, equated with the *Ofanim.* Cf. Ezek. 10:13.

49. These graphic measurements represent an extreme form of rabbinic mystical speculation called *shi'ur qomah,* which literally measures God's height and limbs in proportions conceived as immense. See Cohen, *ibid.* (above, n. 45).

50. This is not a mere repetition of Throne mysticism, mentioned above. Here the question relates to the role of the throne in the creation process. See Rashi to Gen. 1:2, and MT 93:5.

51. One text (*Merkabah Shelemah,* ed. Akiva Parush [Jerusalem, 1921; reprint ed., Jerusalem, 1971]) adds "excellence" (*ma'alati*) to the list. This reading is authenticated by the citation of our text in *Sefer Seror ha-mor* (*toledot*), which includes a citation of 1 Kings 10:19, *There were six steps (ma'alot) to the throne.* All of the terms here have a technical significance in mystical speculation. In the translation "measurement," I follow Scholem, *Major Trends,* 71.

52. Here taken as God's physical dimensions.

53. See above, chap. 6, n. 48.

CHAPTER ELEVEN

1. "Righteousness" (*ṣedaqah*) is taken in rabbinic and later Hebrew to mean charity. For the theme of this paragraph see B. BB 9a–10b. R. Jose's statement is from B. Shab 118b.

2. For a comparison of Solomon with David, see above, on 1:7.

3. It is difficult to discern why this verse is attributed to David. Perhaps Ps. 1:1 is intended.

4. This is derived from the Hebrew of *Assuredly,* which reads literally "hand upon hand" (a gesture indicating a sworn oath).

5. See above, chap. 2, n. 4, for the relationship of R. Eliezer and R. Joshua. The parable of R. Joḥanan in the preceding paragraph is to be compared with B. Ber 61a.

6. This reasoning is based on the hermeneutic device of analogy from verbal

congruity. Because both verses use the same Hebrew words, it is assumed that they share the same legal context. See above, chap. 10, n. 32, for more on this hermeneutic method.

7. By paying her less than he had promised.

8. See B. Suk 52a, and for more on the inclination to evil cf. *Torah Shelemah,* ed. M. M. Kasher (New York, 1958) to Gen. 8:21 nn. 100–01.

9. *Yoreh* ("satisfies"), from the root *rwh* ("to be saturated"), is interpreted as being derived from the root *yrh* ("to shoot [an arrow]"). Hence the one who refrains from teaching is "pierced." Cf. B. Sanh 91b–92a.

10. Usually translated *two nations,* etc. This series of puns and exchanges renders a version of Proverbs which supports 'Ula's contention.

11. Usually translated *I will be gracious to whom I will be gracious.*

12. An anachronism referring to the seventy elders who served with Moses as if they were the rabbinic Sanhedrin (great court) of the Yavnean (post-70 C.E.) era.

13. See Num. 15:38ff. This law immediately precedes the story of Korah's rebellion. Cf. Num. Rabbah 22:7, 18:3 and parallels.

14. The command in Deut. 6:9 just quoted mandates a *mezuzah.*

15. These verses not only show that Korah himself and his company of men were punished but also indicate, by the phrase *their households,* that Korah's wife was even more at fault.

16. Cf. Num. 16:30, *they go down alive to the pit.*

17. Cf. B. Sanh 190b.

18. MM provides no comment on Prov. 11:29–12:19.

CHAPTER TWELVE

1. The kidneys were regarded as the seat of the emotions; cf. B. Ber 61a.

2. Lit., "to him who speaks one thing with his mouth and another in his heart."

3. This interpretation leads directly into Chap. 13, which continues with the exegesis of Prov. 13:20, there being no comments on the intervening verses.

CHAPTER THIRTEEN

1. These parables and the moral drawn from them are also found in ARN (B) chap. 28 and in PRE chap. 25.

2. Rabbi Simeon here understands the verse to say: The mighty devour the tillage of the poor. Rabbi Jose renders it: Some are swept away prior to [formal] judgment.

3. This comment of R. Eliezer is added from the manuscripts.

4. Babylon, Assyria, Greece, and Rome.

5. The verse is usually translated *Neither has the eye seen a God beside You, who works for him* [. . . .]

CHAPTER FOURTEEN

1. The tradition of the three siblings and their three gifts to Israel dates back to the mishnaic era. See Tos Sot 11:8 and the commentary of Lieberman, *TK*, ad loc., 722–23.

2. For more on Miriam's prophecy see Brown, *Birth of the Messiah*, 116 n. 45, and the bibliography cited there, 119ff.

3. The proof of the contention comes from the exegesis of this verse, which follows.

4. Viz., prophecy.

5. MM provides no comment to Prov. 14:3–26.

6. The congregational response to the Sanctification (*qaddish*) prayer. See above, chap. 10, n. 38.

7. A pun: *razon* ("prince") is paired with *raze* ("secrets"). "The Secrets of Torah" may be the title of a specific work of rabbanite mysticism.

8. When he learns of his reward in the world to come.

9. It is a common rabbinic adage that no reign may overlap another. See, e.g., B. Ber 48b, Shab 30a, etc. For more on Moses' final hours see Ginzberg, *Legends*, 3:417–66, 6:146–58, 167–68.

10. "Beck and call," literally, "at Joshua's head." Hunched posture and folded hands indicate servility.

11. The custom of rising early in the morning to offer greetings to one's master, as the Israelites did for Moses and as he did for Joshua, was a common courtesy in the Greco-Roman client–patron relationship. See the next note.

12. Here Joshua has assumed the seated posture of the patron, and Moses the standing posture of the supplicating client. In a large household it would have been entirely possible to overlook one client among many others. For more on the institution of *clientela* see L. Friedlander, *Roman Life and Manners,* trans. L. A. Magnus (New York, 1968) 1:195ff.

13. To show him honor; see Tos Sanh chap. 8, B. 'Er 54b and Ex. 17:12.

14. That is to say, "Ask me not for the reason—I am obeying God's command."

15. That is to say, "Who will intercede before Me to implore mercy for Israel when they have sinned, as Moses had repeatedly done?" For Moses' forgetting of the Torah traditions, cf. Lev Rabbah 13:1.

16. This world and the world to come.

17. The verse is usually translated *Righteousness exalts a nation; but sin is a reproach to any people.* The homilist uses a narrowly particularistic exegesis of this universalist sentiment.

CHAPTER FIFTEEN

1. There is no comment on Prov. 15:1–16.

2. Lit., "his mind was cooled."

3. For more on Solomon's legendary fall from power and his wanderings in poverty, see Ginzberg, *Legends*, 6:300 n. 87, 301 n. 93.

4. Abot 4:1. This Mishnah is part of a series of paradoxes. One would expect a mighty man to conquer others; instead he conquers himself.

5. See chap. 1 above for other comparisons of David with Solomon.

6. The House [of God] is the Jerusalem Temple destroyed in 70 C.E. This fictional account of Vespasian's siege is paralleled in ARN (A) chap. 4 (Goldin, *YJS* 10, 35–38) and in many other Midrashim.

7. "Long live our Lord the Emperor!" The transcription of the Latin is completely corrupt here, but the parallel texts preserve the correct Latin formula.

8. When R. Johanan greeted him as Emperor, Vespasian had not yet been elevated to the throne. Hence the greeting might have exposed Vespasian to a charge of treason. Josephus and Apollonius of Tyana also predicted Vespasian's ascension to imperial power.

9. The identification of Lebanon with the Temple in Jerusalem is a commonplace in rabbinic literature.

10. The author is unaware of the intervening reigns of Galba and Otho during the "year of the four Caesars."

11. Yavneh, lit., "Greektown." The Roman garrison town of Jamnia was referred to by the local Jews as Greektown (*yewani,* a reading preserved in old MSS; see Epstein, *Mabo,* 1225) because of the many Greek-speaking conscripts stationed there. When the Rabbis took over the town, it was renamed Yavneh through a play on words.

12. This is an addition to the end of the Mishnaic tractate Sotah; see Epstein, *Mabo,* 976. I follow Danby's translation here.

CHAPTER SIXTEEN

1. *Halakot,* literally "laws," but the term is used technically to refer to the Mishnah. For the entire passage here, see J. Hor chap. 3, 48c.

2. The text here is somewhat corrupt; *sofer* ("he that counted") is paired with *sofere* ("bookmen, teachers of reading").

3. Technical terminology abounds in this passage. "The Midrashim on law and lore" are exegetical works that subject Scripture to legal (*halakah*) and nonlegal (*aggadah*) interpretation.

4. This parable is similar to the one found in Matt. 22:1–14, and in rabbinic literature in Eccl. Rabbah 9:8 and B. Shab 153a. See Joachim Jeremias, *The Parables of Jesus* (New York, 1973), 187–89.

5. See Gen. 47:1–12, 50:1–14.

6. An anchronism, referring to David's seeking counsel from his elders, before there was any formal court of law called Sanhedrin.

7. See Gen. 18:1ff.

CHAPTER SEVENTEEN

1. Most manuscripts read, "for even an hour." The Hebrew words for "year" (*shanah*) and "hour" (*sha'ah*) vary from each other in only one letter. For the salvific value of the Land of Israel see B. Ket 111a.

2. The verse is usually rendered, *And cleanse the land of His people.*

3. Much like the ones running through the Jewish catacombs at Rome or Bet-She'arim.

4. There is no such verse in the Bible. Perhaps the author had in mind Jer. 16:15, *And I will bring them back upon their land.* Or this may be a conflation of Ezek. 37:21 and 37:23.

5. *Leech* (*'aluqah*) is taken to refer to the insatiable maw of Gehenna.

6. 'Ed 2:10.

7. See above, chap. 2, n. 4.

8. Viz., "dead" to the obligations of Torah law incumbent upon Jews.

9. This leads directly to the comment on 19:1. It is the style of MM to link successive chapters in this fashion; see above, chap. 6, n. 48. There is no comment on 17:2–18:24.

CHAPTER NINETEEN

1. See Gen. 13:16.

2. This is now found as part of Ab 6:4–5, a late liturgical addition called *Qinyan Torah,* dating from the same time as MM.

3. Following the manuscripts and *Qinyan Torah*; the primary text, corrupt here, reads "length of lips" (*'arikhat sefatayim*). For the numbers thirty, twenty-four, and forty-eight for kingship, priesthood, and Torah, see the commentary of Judah Goldin, *The Living Talmud* (New York, 1957), 230–32.

4. B. BM 85a.

5. See 2 Sam. 13–19:11.

6. See 1 Kings 1:5–2:25.

7. See Esther 3:2–3.

8. Cf. Song Rabbah 2:15, Song Zuta 2:15, Exod. Rabbah 22:1.

9. Cf. Lev. Rabbah 36:2.

10. The verse is usually translated, *While the sun lasts, may his name endure—Yinnon* being regarded as a verb, "to endure, to continue."

CHAPTER TWENTY

1. Inverting the syntax of the Hebrew, so that the subject becomes the object, and vice versa.

2. B. Ber 57a, and see Sanh 70a.

3. Translation, according to W. Gesenius (*A Hebrew and English Lexicon to the Old Testament* [Oxford: Oxford University Press, 1906]), of the seven Hebrew terms: *aryeh* (Gen. 49:9), *ari* (Num. 23:24), *kefir* (Judg. 14:5), *labi* (Num. 23:24), *layish* (Isa. 30:6), *shahal* (Ps. 91:13), and *shahas* (Job 28:8). Cf. ARN (B) chap. 43, ARN (A) chap. 39; B. Sanh 95a.

4. Lit., "erected a fence around their words." Cf. Mek Ba-Ḥodesh 4 (p. 215) and parallels.

5. See Ezek. 1:10.

6. For this motif cf. Gen. Rabbah 60:3 and parallels.

7. The Hebrew text is corrupt in this last line, "I will create you a clean heart . . . he wished," and is here emended ad sensum.

8. This odd reading of scriptural geography is taken from Song Rabbah 1:1 (10); cf. MT 72:2, B. Meg 11a.

9. There is no midrash to Prov. 20:10–30.

CHAPTER TWENTY-ONE

1. For this notion see B. Suk 49b.

2. Pe'ah 8:9.

3. The passage in Deut. refers generally to the observance of the commandments of the Torah.

4. The Hebrew word used here for *success* (*ṣedaqah*) is the same as the word for "righteousness" and "charity." Cf. B. BB 9b.

5. The "honor of the sages" being rabbinic lore.

6. He ascended Mount Sinai into the heavenly realm to receive the Torah. For the entire paragraph, see Midrash Tannaim p. 227, Lev. Rabbah 31:5 and parallels.

7. The purpose of the interdict was to limit the daughter's suitors to those from the "proper" areas. See Lieberman, *Greek in Jewish Palestine*, 10–12.

8. The father-in-law of Moses.

9. "To come" is a technical term for becoming a proselyte. See Lieberman, ibid., 80 n. 98.

10. The account of the war, Exod. 17:8–16, immediately precedes Exod. 18:1.

11. It is not clear why this verse is attributed to David; but cf. chap. 1, n. 57.

12. There is no comment to Prov. 21:24–31.

CHAPTER TWENTY-TWO

1. For the "hint to the wise," cf. *Scriptores Historiae Augustae*, Tacitus 19:5, "Dictum sapienti sat est."

2. Ab 3:6.

3. The written Hebrew word (*ketiv*) for *excellent things* is written *shilshom* ("day before yesterday, time past"), and was pointed (*qere*) by the Masoretes as *shalishim* (lit., "third officers" or "commanders of three [subordinates]"). Bar Huna interprets Prov. 22:20 in both ways.

4. The first, middle, and last letters of the Hebrew alphabet; cf. Tanḥuma Jethro 10.

5. Reading triplets (*shelishim*) for excellent things (shalishim).

6. Each of these statements echoes the biblical injunction *Do not favor the poor or show deference to the rich* (Lev. 19:15). In other words, in a court of law, justice must be dispensed without fear or favor. Cf. Ket 9:2–3.

7. This anachronistic attribution of the thrice-daily liturgy is found already in B. Ber 26b but may have been adapted here to serve as a polemical attempt to fend off Karaite liturgical reform.

8. See B. Sanh 104b, Song Rabbah 1:5.

9. Sanh 10:2. The evil kings mentioned there are Jeroboam, Ahab, and Manasseh; the commoners are Balaam, Doeg, Ahitophel, and Gehazi. The unknown sages wished also to bar Solomon because of the cynical attitudes expressed in Ecclesiastes (which were perhaps taken to be reflected in Solomon's behavior—see Lev. Rabbah 19:2, which outlines his sins). When Ecclesiastes was admitted to the scriptural canon, it became clear that Solomon had a place in the world to come. See Saul Lieberman, "Notes on Chapter One of Ecclesiastes Rabbah," *Studies in Mysticism and Religion Presented to Gershom G. Scholem*, 3 vols. (Hebrew) (Jerusalem: Magnes Press, 1967), 2:163–65.

10. An unusual division within the Godhead. See Gershom Scholem, *Major Trends in Jewish Mysticism* (New York: Schocken, 1961), 377 n. 127, and E. E. Urbach, *The Sages* (Hebrew) (Jerusalem: Magnes Press, 1975), 50f. The epithet "Holy, praised be He" is abbreviated in the Hebrew text and might possibly also be rendered, "Omnipresent, praised be He."

CHAPTER TWENTY-THREE

1. For this theme, see B. Pes 87b; Mek Beshallaḥ (p. 178); ARN (B) chap. 43; ARN (A) chap. 41. For flying letters, cf. B. ʿAZ 18a.

2. For the relationship between these two sages, see above, chap. 2, n. 4. For the calculations which follow see Ginzberg, *Legends* 6:58 n. 300, 59 n. 303.

3. A measure of roasted barley offered daily in the Temple between Passover and Pentecost (see Lev. 23:10–21). The *omer* offering ceased with the destruction of the Temple in 70 C.E., as did the other Temple rituals listed below.

4. See Lev. 24:5–9.

5. Wine libations accompanying the sacrifices and water libations offered on the Feast of Tabernacles.

6. See Exod. 28.

7. See Exod. 30:11–16.

8. See Num. 28:26.

9. See above, n. 5.

10. See Exod. 40:15, 27:20.

11. See Num. 28.

12. See, e.g., Num. 7:17ff. The commentary on Hag. 1:6 and Hab. 3:19 here is found also in Tanḥuma Teṣawweh 13 and parallels. For a similar list of consequences of the Temple's destruction, see Sot 9:12ff.

13. There is no comment on Prov. 23:6–23.

14. The Hebrew prefix *way-* ("and") is homonymous with the exclamation *way* ("Woe!"). It occurs approximately thirteen times in these verses, the rabbis using the popular number thirteen to emphasize the calamity. See Gen. Rabbah 36:4 and parallels for more on this motif.

15. For this play on words, cf. Lev. Rabbah 12:1.

CHAPTER TWENTY-FOUR

1. There is no comment on 23:33–24:9 nor on 24:11–22.

2. That is, in any of the commandments; cf. B. Ber 63a.

3. See above, chap. 1, nn. 51–52. Without reviewing, the disciple will forget even the catchwords by which Oral Torah is organized.

CHAPTER TWENTY-FIVE

1. The homily on Moses' temper is interrupted by this homily on Prov. 25:1 and Eccl. 11:9. The latter homily is found in ARN (A) chap. 1 (Goldin, *YJS 10*, 5ff.) and parallels.

2. The strap with which court-administered lashes are inflicted; in other words, Solomon seems to recommend complete religious and social anarchy.

3. The Hebrew verb he‘tiq means "to move," hence also "to remove, to copy, to move from one meaning or one tongue to another (i.e., to translate or explicate)."

4. That is to say, do not refuse to admit that your opponent's argument or opinion is more valid than your own.

5. Cf. B. Ta 8b, P. Ta 3:5 (66c).

6. This verse is applied to these two sages for their dangerous mystical speculations. See B. Ḥag 14b, Tos Ḥag 2:3, P. Ḥag 2:1 (77b).

7. R. Abbahu evidently interpreted mefiṣ (lit., "disperser," usually translated "maul, war club" and regarded as a synonym of mappeṣ [Jer. 51:20], "shatterer = war club") as meaning "spear."

CHAPTER TWENTY-SIX

1. An Arabicized (al-Iskandari) spelling of "Alexandri."

2. A Mercurius was a stone statue of the god Hermes that was set up at a crossroads. The statues were found throughout the Roman world. Each pagan passerby would cast a stone at the statue, which would eventually result in a mound of stones honoring the god. The Rabbis considered this a form of idolatry. See Tos AZ 6:15.

3. For the paragraphs on the ten dotted passages of the Bible, see Sif Num. 69 (pp. 64–65), ARN (A) chap. 34 (Goldin, YJS 10, 138–39) and parallels. See, too, Romain Butin, The Ten Nequdoth of the Torah (New York: KTAV, 1969) and Lieberman, Hellenism in Jewish Palestine, 43–46.

4. The dotting therefore indicates that one must read between the lines of Scripture to elicit the true meaning of the verse.

5. As God ruled in Sarah's favor in the second case (Gen. 21), so God must have ruled in her favor in the first case (Gen. 16); hence the dotting.

6. The Hebrew particle marks the direct object, flock.

7. Joseph, who stored up the produce of the seven years of plenty to feed the world during the seven years of famine (Gen. 41).

8. For Second Passover, see M. Pes 9:1–14. For the particular understanding of long (reḥoqah) as meaning "not present," see M. Pes 9:2.

9. Thus Lot was aware of committing incest with his eldest daughter. He nevertheless got drunk again the next night and was subsequently aware of the incest he committed then, also.

10. The verse reads literally, "a tenth part, a tenth part"; the duplication might lead one to the unwarranted assumption that a double tithe is called for here, hence the dotting.

11. The entire passage (Num. 10:35–36) is enclosed within inverted letters nun. See Lieberman, Hellenism, 41 n. 28, which disucsses this passage. Cf. the discussion in Journal of Biblical Literature 93 (1974), 348–55.

12. Modern Hebrew Bibles dot the word following the proper noun Nophah.

13. The homily here returns to Esau's words of deceit (Gen. 27:41) mentioned above, before the digression on the ten dotted passages in the Bible.

14. As long as the voice of Jacob is heard studying Torah, Jacob (Israel) will prevail; otherwise Israel will be subjugated to the hand of Esau.

CHAPTER TWENTY-SEVEN

1. There is no comment on Prov. 27:3–16.
2. A weight of gold or silver worth one hundred common shekels.
3. Pe'ah 1:1. For corner crop see Lev. 19:9; for first fruits see Deut. 26:1–12; for the pilgrimage offering see Deut. 16:16–17.
4. The reflection of the gazer. The Hebrew of both the biblical text and the rabbinic commentary is obscure.
5. The verse does not actually refer to Israel as "herds," although the notion is clearly implied. The verse is repeated immediately below. Perhaps Isa. 40:11, or Jer. 31:9, or another verse with the "herd" imagery is called for here, although such readings are not attested in the manuscripts.

CHAPTER TWENTY-EIGHT

1. The explanation of the first part of the verse is added from the manuscript readings. The latter part of the verse, *a rich man,* also follows the manuscripts and the Masoretic text.
2. Ab 4:10.
3. Latin *as,* a small Roman coin, 1/24 of a denar. The saying of R. Aqiba is found in ARN (A) chap. 3 and parallels.

CHAPTER TWENTY-NINE

1. There is no further comment on Prov. 29.

CHAPTER THIRTY

1. Causing him to speak God's word.
2. *The throne of the Lord*—here interpreted as the throne in heaven.
3. Usually translated "man's"; cf. B. Sanh 70b.
4. For another version of this entire poem see PesDRK (pp. 8–9). The identification of Israel with God's son is also found above, chap. 6, at n. 3.
5. See above, chap. 17, n. 5.
6. A pun: the Hebrew *geber be-ʿalmah* ("a man with a maiden") is read as the Aramaic *gebar be-ʿolma* ("a rooster in the world"); the Hebrew root *gbr* also translates to "rooster" in Mishnaic Hebrew, a shift from its biblical meaning.
7. Gen. 16:1–16, 21:8–21.
8. Edom stands for Rome (and later for Byzantium).
9. This verse is out of order here and is incorrectly joined with 30:33, as though the latter verse listed the four items spoken of in 30:29. The error is presumably the fault of a scribe.
10. That is, he who utilizes the elementary knowledge (his "mother's milk")

acquired in his youth for subsequent advanced study of Torah will gain most profit ("butter") from the latter.

11. He will learn enough to be able to render decisions in the difficult matter of menstrual unfitness.

12. He will learn enough to sit on the High Court, which has jurisdiction over capital cases.

CHAPTER THIRTY-ONE

1. For the homily about Solomon's marriage ceremonies and the aftermath, cf. B. Sanh 70b and Lev. Rabbah 12:5.

2. Cf. Ber. 1:3, "It is the custom of kings to rise at the third hour."

3. A pun: *peninim* ("rubies") is paired with *lifnai lifnim* ("innermost [Chamber]"). *Lifnai lifnim* usually refers to the Holy of Holies in the Jerusalem Temple, but it is also found in Gnostic literature, where it refers to the heavenly seat of pure and salvific knowledge.

4. This is the earliest known reference to the custom of holding study sessions on Sabbath afternoons.

5. The Benediction of "Separation," recited at the close of the Sabbath or holy day.

6. *Maqom* means both "place" and "the Omnipresent" (= God). R. Meir's wife thus tells him that his sons have gone to God (i.e., have died), while withholding the plain truth from him until the Sabbath has ended and he has eaten. Only then can R. Meir appropriately give way to his grief, since mourning is prohibited on the Sabbath.

7. An indirect way of saying, "Surely you know full well that he is obligated."

8. And not "prey" or "leaf" as in other passages. The homilist establishes its meaning here by quoting other proof-verses in which the term appears; cf. B. 'Er 18b, Sanh 108b. For the preceding homily on food and Torah study, see B. Ḥag 12b, 'AZ 3b.

9. Usually translated "plucked off."

10. Presumably against cursing God, against theft, regarding the duty to institute courts of law, against incest, against bloodshed, and against idolatry. These six added to Noah's commandment constitute the seven Noachide laws. See, e.g., Maimonides, *Code, Book of Judges,* Kings 9:1. See PesDRK (pp. 202–04) for this homily, which continues here to p. 123.

11. In a generation not as evil as his, Noah would not have seemed so good a man. See Gen. 6:9, *Noah was a righteous man; he was blameless in his age.*

12. Added from manuscripts and parallels. Midrashic homily allows the "woman" of Proverbs to be interpreted as the man Moses.

13. Midrash Mishle thus concludes with praise of wisdom and Torah, and of God, who gave both of them to Israel.

INDEX OF SUBJECTS

. . .

151

INDEX OF RABBINIC AUTHORITIES

· · ·

INDEX OF PRIMARY TEXTS,
WITH ABBREVIATIONS

．　　．　　．

Biblical Passages

Rabbinic Sources

New Testament

Hellenistic Sources

INDEX OF MODERN AUTHORS

. . .